Everyday Spanish

About the book

This book is a publication of the Language Link Project. The parent organization of the Language Link Project is called Linked Humanity.

The purpose of Linked Humanity is to create affordable educational materials for a global audience. It currently has two focus areas:

- Language Learning (managed by Language Link)
- Technology Learning (managed by Technology Link)

This is the first book in our Everyday series, which focuses on teaching you common phrases and vocabulary with their cultural context. We also have "Everyday Mandarin/Arabic/Portuguese/Urdu" in the works, and they are expected to be ready in the next few months.

The audio for the book content is available for free on our YouTube channel called **"Language Link - Americas"**. You should be able to locate the channel by visiting our website at www.linkedhumanity.org.

Acknowledgments

All the translation and explanation notes for this book were created by Mariana Huerta.

ISBN 978-1-7333632-0-4

Table of Contents

Preface

This book aims to teach you Spanish in an easy and fun way. The "Introduction" section gives an overview of various Spanish dialects and the differences between them. The "Language Concepts" chapter walks you through the Spanish alphabets with a focus on hard to pronounce letters as well as letters that are treated differently in Spanish compared to English. It also gives a high-level overview of Spanish grammar, which includes sentence structure and tenses. We tried to keep it light so that you get the basics without getting overwhelmed.

Chapters 1 - 10 teach you common phrases and related vocabulary. Each phrase has a notes section that contains short explanations about the phrase. This explanation can be about the cultural context, pronunciation of certain words, or to explain the grammar rule behind the phrase.

To keep things interesting, each chapter starts with an inspirational quote from a famous person and its Spanish translation and ends with a short essay with both English and Spanish side-by-side. There is also a "Read and Recall" practice exercise section at the end of each chapter to let you practice all the phrases and vocabulary you learned in the chapter.

The book contains grammar tables following the main chapters. This information can help you form different types of sentences, such as past or future tense. At the end is a short English to Spanish dictionary.

Learning a language requires consistent practice. It does not have to be a lot, but it has to be continuous over the long term. We hope this book makes it easy for you to practice regularly while staying engaged.

Introduction

"A journey of a thousand miles begins with a single step."

"Un viaje de mil millas comienza con un solo paso."

Lao Tzu
Chinese philosopher
(601 - 531 BC)

Spanish is one of the most widely spoken languages on Earth and a member of the Romance language family. It evolved from the variation of Vulgar Latin that was spoken in the Iberian Peninsula after the fall of the Western Roman Empire. It is related to other Western European languages such as French, Italian, Portuguese, and Romanian.

Due to the Spanish Conquest over much of what is now known as Latin America in the western hemisphere, Spanish is not only spoken in Spain but is widespread throughout the 33 Latin American countries. It is also spoken by large Latin American communities in the United States and is rapidly gaining influence as the Latino population in the U.S. grows. Since Spanish has been exported to such a broad region of the world, it has taken on unique characteristics over time in different areas of Latin America, as well as in Spain itself. The noticeable differences in spoken Spanish among the different regions of the Spanish-speaking world can be thought of as dialects considering how much they have diverged.

The most pronounced difference in spoken Spanish is between European Spanish and Latin American Spanish. In addition to differences in slang and vernacular, the main distinguishing feature of European Spanish is its signature ceceo. Ceceo is the phenomenon where the z sound and soft c sound is pronounced like a th, while the s is pronounced like it is in English. For the most part, this speech pattern is widely used in Spain, whereas Latin America follows a seseo speech pattern. Seseo is where z, s, and soft c are all pronounced like the s sound is pronounced in English.

Although ceceo is used throughout Spain, and seseo is commonplace in Latin America, there can be exceptions to this trend. For example, in parts of Southern Spain, one will hear the seseo used, much like in Latin America. Linguistic scholars believe that Latin America's use of seseo rather than ceceo is likely rooted in the fact that the majority of Spaniards who colonized the Americas were from Southern Spain, where the seseo speech pattern is more prevalent.

Furthermore, the modern Spanish we hear today has not only been influenced by language patterns from Spain but also by the indigenous languages of the Americas encountered during colonization. In Mexican Spanish, for example, one can find many nahuatlísmos used in everyday language. These are words directly derived from the language of the Aztecs, Nahuatl, that have found their way into Mexican Spanish. Not only have indigenous languages influenced Latin American Spanish, but later waves of immigrants from other parts of the world have also influenced Spanish with their native languages.

The Spanish spoken in today's world is a complex language with a variety of cultural influences to thank for its richness. It can often vary from country to country and even within the regions of a country. That is part of what makes it so fascinating to study Spanish and become a part of the global community of speakers of this beautiful language.

Language Concepts

"If you can't explain it simply, you don't understand it well enough."

"Si no puedes explicarlo simplemente, no lo entiendes lo suficientemente bien."

Albert Einstein

German-born theoretical physicist

(1879–1955)

Alphabets

Aa a	Bb be	Cc ce	Dd de	Ee e
Ff efe	Gg ge	Hh hache	Ii i	Jj jota
Kk ka	Ll ele	Mm eme	Nn ene	Ññ eñe
Oo o	Pp pe	Qq ku	Rr ere	Ss ese
Tt te	Uu u	Vv ve	Ww doble ve	Xx equis
Yy i griega	Zz zeta			

The chart above contains the basic Spanish alphabet, including the name of each letter. Spanish uses the same 26 letters of the Latin alphabet that English uses, but there is an additional letter "ñ" in the Spanish alphabet. Therefore, there is a total of 27 distinct letters in the Spanish alphabet.

Pronunciation

Difficult consonants

Gg ge	Hh hache	Jj jota
Ññ eñe	Rr ere	Vv ve

These are some letters from the Spanish alphabet that might be tricky for English speakers to pronounce because they are used differently than in English. We will discuss how to pronounce the names and phonetic sounds of each of these letters below:

Gg [ge] - The letter "G" is called "ge" in Spanish. "Ge" is pronounced "h-eh," using a soft g sound rather than a hard g. Note that the soft g sound in Spanish is different from the soft g sound in English. In English, the soft g sound is similar to the English j sound. In Spanish, however, the soft g sound is similar to the h sound in the English words "hair" or "how."

Although the soft g in Spanish is different from the soft g in English, the hard g sound in Spanish is the same as the hard g in English. The hard g sound in Spanish is pronounced like the g sound in the words "gum" or "grow."

Hh [hache] - The letter "H" is called "hache" in Spanish. "Hache" is pronounced "ah-cheh." Note that the h at the beginning of "hache" is silent. The letter h in Spanish is silent in most words, such as "hola" or "hielo."

Jj [jota] - The letter "J" is called "jota" in Spanish. "Jota" is pronounced "hoh-tah." Note that the letter j at the beginning of "jota" is pronounced like the English h sound found in words like "hit" or "has." In Spanish, the j sound is generally pronounced like the h sound in English.

Ññ [eñe] - The letter "Ñ" is called "eñe" in Spanish. "Eñe" is pronounced "en-nyeh." Note that the letter ñ has no equivalent in English. It has its own unique pronunciation, similar to the "nyuh" sound in the English words "canyon" or "minion."

Rr [ere] - The letter "R" is called "ere" in Spanish. "Ere" is pronounced "eh-deh." Note that the letter r in Spanish is not drawn out like the English r in words like "car" or "road," but it is formed by a light tap on the roof of the mouth. The sound made by r in Spanish is similar to the sound made by the letter d or t in English words such as "cadaver" and "elevator."

Vv [ve] - The letter "V" is called "ve" in Spanish. "Ve is pronounced "bh-eh." Note that the letter v in Spanish is not pronounced like v in the English words "love" or "very," but rather it is pronounced like b in the English words "bear" or "bake."

Other consonant sounds

There are a few more important consonants to know in Spanish beyond the ones in the alphabet. They consist of duplicates of one letter or a combination of two letters but are used as commonly in Spanish as many single consonants of the alphabet are. They are listed below:

Consonant sound	Name	Usage in Spanish	English equivalent
Ll, ll	elle ("eh-yeh")	pollo, llorar	y sound in "yogurt" and "yam"
Rr, rr	erre ("eh-rheh")	carro, tierra	r sound in "road" and "rhetoric"
Ch, ch	che ("ch-eh")	techo, chorizo	ch sound in "cheese" and "reach"

Vowels

The Spanish alphabet has the same five vowels as the English alphabet. However, they are pronounced a bit differently than in English. Vowels in Spanish are pronounced like the short vowel pronunciation (ah, eh, ee, o, oo) in English but are not pronounced like long vowels (ay, ee, eye, oh, yoo) in English. Otherwise, they are quite similar between Spanish and English. Refer to the table below for Spanish vowels, their pronunciation, and usage.

Vowel	Name	Usage in Spanish	English equivalent
a	a ("ah")	cama, pera	a in "card" and "fall"
e	e ("eh")	vela, ser	e in "sketch" and "tell"
i	i ("ee")	pintar, silla	ee in "see" and "feel"
o	o ("oh")	corta, todo	o in "sore" and "for"
u	u ("oo")	pura, salud	oo in "pool" and "too"

Grammar

Soy vs. Estoy

A common dilemma one might have when learning to speak Spanish is the question of when to use the verb "ser" versus "estar." It is mostly found in the usage of "soy" and "estoy," the first person present indicative forms of these verbs, respectively. Translated to English, "soy" and "estoy" both mean "I am." This is because "ser" and "estar" both translate to mean "to be" in English. However, in Spanish, these verbs represent two different forms of being - one represents a permanent state of being, and the other represents a temporary state of being. "Soy" is the more permanent state of being and is usually used to describe something with lasting attributes. For example, "soy alta" means "I am tall," which describes an attribute of mine that remains constant and is relatively permanent. Conversely, "estoy" is the more temporary state of being and is used to describe temporary attributes as well as the state of being at a certain location.

For example, "estoy cansada," meaning "I am tired," represents a temporary state of being tired, which can change easily. In addition, "estoy en la escuela," meaning "I am at school," will always use the temporary "estoy" because locations are always represented with this temporary state of being. Knowing the key difference in usage and meaning between "ser" and "estar" is important in learning Spanish and will save a lot of confusion in the future.

Adjectives

Another hallmark of Spanish grammar is the placement of adjectives after their objects in a sentence. In English, one would place the adjective before its object, such as in the phrase "it is a sunny day." However, in Spanish, this would translate to "es un día soleado." "Día," meaning "day," comes before the word "soleado," or "sunny," being used to describe it. The order of adjectives and their objects in Spanish is an important difference between Spanish and English.

Gender

Words in Spanish can have one of three genders: masculine, feminine, or neuter. Examples of each type of word can be found below:

Masculine	el carro	el gato	el árbol
Feminine	la flor	la escuela	la manzana
Neuter	lo mejor	lo nuevo	lo tuyo

Notice the difference in the article "the" before each type of word. For masculine words, the masculine form of "the," "el," is used. Feminine words use "la," and neuter words tend to use "lo."

Just as the gender of an article should match the gender of the word it modifies, the gender of an adjective should also match the word it describes. Below is the previous table of words updated with adjectives matching the gender of the words:

Masculine	el carro **nuevo**	el gato **grande**	el árbol **viejo**
Feminine	la flor **bonita**	la escuela **grande**	la manzana **roja**
Neuter	lo mejor	lo nuevo	lo tuyo

Notice that "gato" and "escuela" are both modified by the neuter adjective "grande." Neuter adjectives can modify either masculine or feminine words and remain the same. Also notice that the neuter words do not have adjectives to describe them. This is because neuter words tend to be adjectives themselves. They can become gendered when they are used to describe words with the masculine or feminine gender, but when they are used as nouns in a sentence, they are neuter and treated as such with the neuter article "lo."

Number

Adjectives and articles must not only match the words they modify in gender, but they must also match in number. Words can be singular or plural, and the articles and adjectives that describe them can also vary from singular to plural.

Singular	**el** pájaro **verde**	**la** camisa **suave**	**el** tren **largo**
Plural	**las** frutas **frescas**	**los** perros **lindos**	**las** hormigas **pequeñas**

Notice that the articles and adjectives describing both the singular and plural words are bolded in the table above.

First, second, and third person
In Spanish, sentences in first, second, and third-person are constructed a bit differently than in English. In English, verbs stay the same as or very similar to each other across the first, second, and third person.

Example: I eat, you eat, she eats

Spanish, however, requires verbs to be conjugated from the infinitive form of the verb. The infinite form of any verb in Spanish translates as "to [verb]" in English. Conjugations are just the different forms of this root verb depending on person, tense, and number.

Example: correr (to run), dormir (to sleep), llorar (to cry)

The Spanish verbs above are in their infinitive form. Notice that infinitive forms of a verb tend to end in the letter "r". This is a good way to tell if a verb is in the infinitive form. However, many times, the verb needs to be conjugated in order to be used in a sentence.

Example:
cantar (to sing)
yo canto (I sing), tú cantas (you sing), él canta (he sings)

Notice how the verb endings for each form of "to sing" are different when used in the first, second, or third person. This is a conjugation of the verb "cantar" in the singular present first, second, and third-person tenses.

Past, present, and future tense
In addition to first, second, and third-person forms of verbs, there are also different tenses that verbs can vary across. The main ones to focus on are the simple past, present, and future tenses. The following tables provide simple past, present, and future tense forms of the verb "estar" (to be) in the first, second, and third person:

Past:
yo estuve (I was), tú estuviste (you were), ella estuvo (she was), nosotros estuvimos (we were), ustedes estuvieron (you all were), ellos estuvieron (they were)

Present:
yo estoy (I am), tú estas (you are), él está (he is), nosotros estamos (we are), ustedes están (you all are), ellos están (they are)

Future:
yo estaré (I will be), tú estarás (you will be), ella estará (she will be), nosotros estaremos (we will be), ustedes estarán (you all will be), ellos estarán (they will be)

These are all examples of the same verb in different forms depending on whether it is in the past, present, or future tense and first, second, or third person. Notice that the infinitive verb "estar" has its ending removed, leaving it with the root "est-" for conjugation. Different endings are added to this root depending on the conjugation.

Comparing Spanish and Portuguese
As many speakers and learners of Spanish may notice, Spanish and other Romance languages such as Portuguese share many similarities, especially when it comes to written language. Although Spanish and Portuguese sound very different when they are spoken, they appear quite similar when written. This is referred to as the mutual intelligibility between the two languages. When reading a phrase in Portuguese, a Spanish speaker might be able to follow a good portion of its meaning due to how similar words and sentence structures are between the two languages.

1
Greetings

"Do I not destroy my enemies when I make them my friends?"

"¿No destruyo a mis enemigos cuando los hago mis amigos?"

Abraham Lincoln
President of United States
(1809 – 1865)

1

Hello

Hola

Vocabulary

greetings - saludos
welcome - la bienvenida
reception - recepción
flowers - las flores
personal - personal
authentic - auténtico
sincere - sincero/a
genuine - genuino
stranger - desconocido/a
mindful - consciente

Notes

Pronunciation: The "h" in "hola" is silent, resulting in the pronunciation "o-la"

2

Good Morning

Buenos días

Buenos - good
días - day

Vocabulary

dawn - madrugada
yawn - bostezo
stretch - tramo
sunrise - la salida del sol
ready - listo/a
start - empezar
in a hurry - apurado
mirror - espejo

Notes

Pronunciation: "días" is pronounced "DEE-ahs" due to accented i.
Culture: Any time you enter a small establishment (restaurant, store, etc.) in Latin America it is customary to announce one's presence by saying "buenos días", "buenas tardes" or "buenas noches".

3

Good afternoon

Buenas tardes

Buenas - good	tardes - afternoon

Vocabulary

12 o clock - las doce del día	**sunshine** - la luz del sol
day - día	**doze off** - dormitar
noon - medio día	**drowsy** - soñoliento/a
sunny - soleado	**nap** - siesta

Notes

Grammar: "Buenas" is the feminine plural form of "bueno," which means "good." This adjective takes the feminine plural form because it describes "tardes," which is feminine and plural. Adjectives in Spanish must match their objects in gender and number.

4

Good evening

Buenas noches

Buenas - good	noches - night

Vocabulary

shade - sombra	**horizon** - horizonte
getting dark - oscurecer	**sky** - cielo
dusk - la anochecida	**colorful** - colorido
sunset - atardecer	**amazing** - asombroso

Notes

Grammar: To say "good evening" in Spanish, one says "buenas noches." There is no distinct translation for "evening" in Spanish, so "noches" is used, although it means "night." "Buenas noches" is commonly used to mean either "good evening" or "good night."

5

Good night

Hasta mañana

Hasta - until
mañana - tomorrow

Vocabulary

twilight - crepúsculo	**dark** - oscuro
becoming night - anochecer	**blind** - ciego/a
moon - luna	**scary** - espantoso
night - noche	**scared** - espantado/a

Notes

Culture: This is usually used before going to bed

Talk: "Buenas noches" is the literal translation of "good night" and is equal to "hasta mañana." Since it can also mean "good evening," we introduce "hasta mañana" as an additional translation of "good night."

6

Goodbye

Adiós/Chao

Adiós - formal/permanent
Chao - informal/temporary

Vocabulary

short stay - estancia corta	**departure** - partida
pack - empacar	**flight time** - tiempo de vuelo
lock - cerradura	**hurry up** - darse prisa
farewell - despedida	**take me to** - llévame a

Notes

Talk: "Adiós" and "chao" are two common ways to say goodbye. Adiós is formal while "chao" is informal. "Adiós" is also more permanent than "chao." Someone going on a long trip would say "adiós". Two friends saying goodbye after chatting might say "chao."

7

See you later

Hasta luego

Hasta - until	luego - later

Vocabulary

when - cuando	**before** - antes
after - después	**previous** - anterior
next - siguiente	**last** - último
near future - futuro cercano	**past** - pasado

Notes

Pronunciation: The word "hasta" has a silent h, so it is pronounced "ah-stah"

Talk: This is a more informal way to say goodbye to someone

8

Nice to see you

Mucho gusto

Mucho - much	gusto - pleasure

Vocabulary

contact - contacto	**charming** - encantador/a
meet - conocer	**smile** - sonrisa
shake hands - darse las manos	**people** - gente
first time - primera vez	**familiarity** - familiaridad
pleasure - placer	**rude** - grosero/a
pleasant - agradable	**pride** - orgullo

Notes

Grammar: "Mucho gusto" literally translates to "much pleasure (to meet you)" and is often used in the context of meeting someone

9

Same here

Yo también/Igualmente

Yo - me
también - as well
Igualmente - equally

Vocabulary

equal - igual
I agree - estoy de acuerdo
me too - yo también
same - mismo
similar - parecido
resemblance - semejanza
I disagree - no estoy de acuerdo
opposite - opuesto

Notes

Pronunciation: The g in "igualmente" doesn't make a g sound, but a w sound since it is combined with u and a. "Igualmente" is pronounced "ee-wahl-men-teh"

10

Thank you

Gracias

Vocabulary

appreciate - apreciar
be grateful - estar agradecido/a
thank you very much - muchas gracias
no thanks to you - no gracias a ti
principled - de principios
to thank - agradecer
formal - formal
informal - informal
impolite - descortés
best - superior

Notes

Grammar: Another common way to thank someone is to say "muchas gracias" which means "thank you very much." Because "gracias" is a plural feminine noun, "muchas" is in its plural feminine form in order to describe it.

11

You are welcome

De nada

De - of	nada - nothing

Vocabulary

no worries - no te preocupes	**polite** - cortés
no problem - no hay problema	**decent** - decente
with pleasure - con placer	**graceful** - agraciado/a
formality - formalidad	**well-mannered** - bien portado/a
easy-going - buena onda	**customer service** - servicio al cliente

Notes

Culture: Most standard, formal way to say "you're welcome"

12

How are you?

¿Cómo estás?/¿Qué tal?

Cómo - how	¿Qué tal? - how's it going?
estás - are you	

Vocabulary

condition - condición	**mental** - mental
to feel - sentir	**emotional** - emocional
well-being - bienestar	**spiritual** - espiritual
state - estado	**calm** - sereno
physical - material	**collected** - compuesto

Notes

Talk: "¿Cómo estás?" is more formal whereas "¿qué tal?" is more informal and equivalent to asking "what's up?" or "how's it going?"

13

I am fine. And you?

Estoy bien. ¿Y usted? (¿Y tú?)

Estoy - I am	usted - you (formal)
bien - well	tú - you (informal)
Y - and	

Vocabulary

fine - bien	**great** - genial
good - bueno	**super** - súper
better - mejor	**paradise** - paraíso
excellent - excelente	**hell** - infierno

Notes

Grammar: The "usted" form of "you" is the formal way to address someone, while "tú" is the more informal way to address someone.

14

I am not fine

No estoy bien

No - not	bien - well
estoy - I am	

Vocabulary

bad - mal	**think** - pensar
worse - peor	**thoughts** - pensamientos
worst - lo peor	**depressed** - deprimido/a
stressed - estresado/a	**fever** - fiebre
upset - trastornado	**headache** - dolor de cabeza

Notes

Grammar: "No" can mean both "no" and "not" in Spanish.

15

Have a good day

Ten un buen día

Ten - have	buen - good
un - a	día - day

Vocabulary

enjoy - disfrutar	**enjoyment** - gozo
happy - feliz	**eventful** - memorable
joyful - alegre	**blessed** - bendito/a
fun - divertido	**cursed** - maldito/a

Notes

Grammar: "Ten" is the imperative form of the verb "tener," meaning "to have." "Buen" is a neuter adjective, so its form remains the same regardless of the gender of "día."

16

Have a good weekend

Ten un buen fin de semana

Ten - have	fin - end
un - a	de - of
buen - good	semana - week

Vocabulary

day off - día de descanso	**process my mail** - procesar mi correo
useful - útil	**do nothing** - hacer nada
make use of - hacer uso de	**catch up on sleep** - alcanzar el sueño
pending errands - el quehacer pendiente	

Notes

Grammar: "Un" is used to describe "fin de semana" because it is masculine and singular like the word "fin."

17

Long time no see

Mucho tiempo sin verle (verte)

Mucho - much
tiempo - time
sin - without
verle - seeing you (formal)
verte - seeing you (informal)

Vocabulary

ages - siglos
duration - duración
always - siempre
frequently - frecuentemente
occasionally - de vez en cuando
sometimes - a veces
never - nunca
avoid - evitar

Notes

Grammar: "Verle" is the formal way to say "see you." "Verte" is informal.

18

I am glad to see you again

Me da gusto verle (verte) de nuevo

Me da - it gives me
gusto - pleasure
verle - to see you (formal)
verte - to see you (informal)
de nuevo - once again

Vocabulary

bump into - encontrarse con
chance encounter - encuentro casual
surprise - sorpresa
unexpected - inesperado/a
suddenly - de repente
again - de nuevo
once again - otra vez
repeat - repetir

Notes

Grammar: "Me da gusto" is a common construction in Spanish. It is used to mean "I am happy/I enjoy" so it is used in this translation.

19

I need to leave now

Necesito irme ahora

Necesito - I need	ahora - now
irme - to leave	

Vocabulary

getting late - volviendo tarde	**immediately** - inmediatamente
door - puerta	**right now** - ahora mismo
entrance - ingreso	**not now** - no ahora
to exit - salir	**some other time** - algún otra vez
windows - ventanas	

Notes

Grammar: "Irme" is a first person form of the "ir," an irregular verb. Its conjugations do not follow regular verb conventions.

20

I hope to see you soon

Espero verle (verte) pronto

Espero - I hope	verte - to see you (informal)
verle - to see you (formal)	pronto - soon

Vocabulary

expectation - expectativa	**fast** - rápido/a
my hopes - mis esperanzas	**instantly** - instantemente
wish - deseo	**quickly** - rápidamente
oath - juramento	**slow** - despacio
word of honor - palabra de honor	**slowly** - pausadamente

Notes

Grammar: "Espero" is the first person singular form of "esperar," meaning to hope or to wait.

Benefits of greetings
Beneficios de los saludos

Greeting people with a smile can help you make new friends.

You must greet people in the mornings, afternoons and evenings.

If you meet someone for the first time, extend your hand for a handshake.

Children learn from their parents, so parents should set a good example by always greeting people with enthusiasm.

If someone is angry, a warm greeting can calm them down. If someone is upset, a kind greeting can change their mood.

In India, people fold their hands together with a slight nod. In Japan, people take a slight bow.

Saludar a las personas con una sonrisa puede ayudar a hacer nuevos amigos.

Debes saludar a las personas por las mañanas, tardes y noches.

Si te encuentras con alguien por primera vez, extiende tu mano para un apretón de manos.

Los niños aprenden de sus padres, por lo que los padres deberían dar un buen ejemplo, siempre saludando a las personas con entusiasmo.

Si alguien está enojado, un saludo cálido puede calmarlo. Si alguien está molesto, un saludo amable puede cambiar su estado de ánimo.

En la India, las personas juntan sus manos con una inclinación ligera. En Japón, la gente hace una leve reverencia.

In some tribal cultures, people touch their nose.

En algunas culturas tribales, la gente se toca la nariz.

It is a good idea to become familiar with the greeting customs of a place you are planning to visit.

Es una buena idea familiarizarse con las costumbres de saludo de un lugar que planea visitar.

This simple step can help you make new friends.

Este paso sencillo puede ayudarte a hacer nuevos amigos.

Read and Recall Meaning

1. Hola

saludos
la bienvenida
recepción
las flores
personal
auténtico
sincero/a
genuino
desconocido/a
consciente

2. Buenos días

madrugada
bostezo
tramo
la salida del sol
listo/a
empezar
apurado
espejo

3. Buenas tardes

las doce del día
día
medio día
soleado
la luz del sol
dormitar
soñoliento/a
siesta

4. Buenas noches

sombra
oscurecer
la anochecida
atardecer
horizonte
cielo
colorido
asombroso

5. Hasta mañana

crepúsculo
anochecer
luna
noche
oscuro
ciego/a
espantoso
espantado/a

6. Adiós/Chao

estancia corta	partida
empacar	tiempo de vuelo
cerradura	darse prisa
despedida	llévame a

7. Hasta luego

cuando	antes
después	anterior
siguiente	último
futuro cercano	pasado

8. Mucho gusto

contacto	encantador/a
conocer	sonrisa
darse las manos	gente
primera vez	familiaridad
placer	grosero/a
agradable	orgullo

9. Yo también/Igualmente

igual	parecido
estoy de acuerdo	semejanza
yo también	no estoy de acuerdo
mismo	opuesto

10. Gracias

apreciar	agradecer
estar agradecido/a	formal
muchas gracias	informal
no gracias a ti	descortés
de principios	superior

11. De nada

no te preocupes	buena onda
no hay problema	cortés
con placer	decente
formalidad	agraciado/a

bien portado/a
servicio al cliente

12. ¿Cómo estás?/¿Qué tal?

condición
sentir
bienestar
estado
material
mental
emocional
espiritual
sereno
compuesto

13. Estoy bien. ¿Y usted? (¿Y tú?)

bien
bueno
mejor
excelente
genial
súper
paraíso
infierno

14. No estoy bien

mal
peor
lo peor
estresado/a
trastornado
pensar
pensamientos
deprimido/a
fiebre
dolor de cabeza

15. Ten un buen día

disfrutar
feliz
alegre
divertido
gozo
memorable
bendito/a
maldito/a

16. Ten un buen fin de semana

día de descanso
útil
hacer uso de
el quehacer pendiente
procesar mi correo
hacer nada
alcanzar el sueño

17. Mucho tiempo sin verle (verte)

siglos
duración
siempre
frecuentemente
de vez en cuando
a veces

nunca	evitar

18. Me da gusto verle (verte) de nuevo

encontrarse con	de repente
encuentro casual	de nuevo
sorpresa	otra vez
inesperado/a	repetir

19. Necesito irme ahora

volviendo tarde	inmediatamente
puerta	ahora mismo
ingreso	no ahora
salir	algún otra vez
ventanas	

20. Espero verle (verte) pronto

expectativa	rápido/a
mis esperanzas	instantemente
deseo	rápidamente
juramento	despacio
palabra de honor	pausadamente

2
Introduce Yourself

"I think, therefore I am."

"Pienso, luego existo."

René Descartes
French Philosopher
(1596 – 1650)

21

What is your name?

¿Cómo te llamas?/¿Cuál es tu nombre?

Cómo - how	Cuál - what
te - you	es - is
llamas - are named	tu nombre - your name

Vocabulary

introduction - introducción	**correct** - correcta
first name - primer nombre	**pronunciation** - pronunciación
last name - apellido	**spelling** - ortografía
nick name - apodo	**meaning** - significado

Notes

Grammar: Cómo se llama/cuál es su nombre are the formal versions of this (usted form)

22

My name is María

Me llamo María / Mi nombre es María

Mi nombre - my name	es - is

Vocabulary

woman - mujer	**information** - información
man - hombre	**appearance** - apariencia
gender - género	**personality** - personalidad
female - hembra	**beliefs** - creencias
male - macho	**religion** - religión

Notes

Pronunciation: The accented "í" in "María" places emphasis on that syllable, resulting in the pronunciation "Mah-REE-ah."
Culture: "Cómo te llamas/me llamo" version is more common.

23

Where are you from?

¿De dónde eres?

De dónde - from where	eres - are you

Vocabulary

nationality - nacionalidad	**born** - nacer
citizen - ciudadano	**grow up** - crecer
ethnicity - etnicidad	**childhood** - niñez
birthplace - lugar de nacimiento	**early schooling** - educación temprana

Notes

Grammar: "Eres" is derived from "ser." It is used here instead of "estás" because "estás" is derived from "estar." "Ser" implies a more permanent state of being, such as a nationality, whereas "estar" implies a temporary state of being, such as a current location.

24

I am from Peru

Soy de Perú

Soy - I am	de - from

Vocabulary

world - mundo	**flag** - bandera
country - país	**nation** - nación
capital - capital	**vote** - voto
population - población	**democracy** - democracia

Notes

Pronunciation: The accented "ú" in "Perú" emphasizes the second syllable in the word, resulting the pronunciation "Pe-ROO"
Grammar: "Soy" is derived from "ser." It is used because it describes a nationality which is more permanent.

25

Which city in Peru?

¿Cuál ciudad en Perú?

Cuál - which
ciudad - city
en - in

Vocabulary

village - pueblo
town - municipio
section - sección
neighbourhood - barrio
community - comunidad
cultural experiences - experiencias culturales
area - área
location - locación
province - provincia
region - región
anthem - himno

Notes

Pronunciation: C is hard before every letter except i or e

26

I live in Lima

Vivo en Lima

Vivo - I live
en - in

Vocabulary

live - vivir
share - compartir
rent - rentar
own - poseer
elevator - elevador
stairs - escaleras
home - hogar
two-story - dos pisos
roof - techo
balcony - balcón

Notes

Culture: Lima is the capital city of Peru. People are more likely to say the city or town they are from than state or province.

How old are you?

¿Cuantos años tienes?

Cuantos - how many
tienes - you have
años - years

Vocabulary

age - edad
infant - infante
baby - bebé
diaper change - cambio de pañal
child - niño
childish - infantil
immature - inmaduro/a
young - joven
teenager - adolescente
legal - legal

Notes

Grammar: "Cuantos" is the plural masculine form of "cuanto," meaning "how much" or "how many."

28

I am twenty years old

Tengo veinte años

Tengo - I have
años - years
veinte - twenty

Vocabulary

adult - adulto
old - viejo
mature - maduro/a
independent - independiente
Mr. - señor
Mrs. - señora
Ms. - señorita
senior - mayor
responsibility - responsabilidad
graduation - graduación

Notes

Pronunciation: The "v" in "veinte" is pronounced with a softer sound closer to a "b" in Spanish.

29

What do you do?

¿Qué haces?

Qué - what	haces - you do

Vocabulary

employ - emplear	**unemployed** - desempleado
employment - empleo	**job** - trabajo
employer - empleador	**to work** - trabajar
employed - empleado	**part-time** - medio tiempo

Notes

Pronunciation: The "h" in "haces" is silent, so it is pronounced "ah-cess."

Grammar: "Qué" has an accent on the last letter when it is used to ask a question. Otherwise it is "que," meaning "which."

30

I am a student

Soy estudiante

Soy - I am	estudiante - a student

Vocabulary

occupation - ocupación	**non-profit** - el no comercial
teacher - maestro/a	**social worker** - trabajador social
engineer - ingeniero/a	**entrepreneur** - emprendedor
military - ejército	**businessman** - empresario
bureaucrat - burócrata	**education** - educación

government official - funcionario del gobierno

Notes

Grammar: "Soy" is used because estudiante is a role (more permanent)

31

Which university do you attend?

¿A qué universidad asistes?

A - to	universidad - university
qué - which	asistes - you attend

Vocabulary

president - presidente
vice-president - vicepresidente
assistant professor - profesor asistente
human resources - recursos humanos
well-spoken - bien hablado
learn - aprender
knowledgeable - enterado
offices - oficinas
dean - decano

Notes

Culture: Most young people tend to stay close to their families during university instead of going far away for school.

32

I attend national university

Asisto a la universidad nacional

Asisto - I attend	universidad - university
a - to	nacional - national
la - the	

Vocabulary

admission - admisión
admission criteria - criterios de admisión
admission officer - oficial de admisión
class size - tamaño de la clase
application deadline - plazo de solicitud
number one - número uno
enroll - inscribir
campus - campus
hostels - hostales
departments - departamentos

Notes

Talk: "La" is used because "universidad" is feminine and singular.

33

What is your major?

¿Cuál es tu especialidad?

Cuál - what	tu - your
es - is	especialidad - speciality

Vocabulary

political science - ciencias políticas	**imagination -** imaginación
medical school - escuela de medicina	**art** - arte
undergrad - licenciatura	**science** - ciencias
master's degree - maestría	**business** - negocios
PhD - doctorado	**engineering** - ingeniería
research - investigación	**humanities** - humanidades

Notes

Grammar: Can also use "su" if using usted form

34

I am studying medicine

Estoy estudiando medicina

Estoy - I am	medicina - medicine
estudiando - studying	

Vocabulary

essay - ensayo	**pass** - pasar
struggle - luchar	**fail** - fallar
final exams - exámenes finales	**brain** - cerebro
easy - fácil	**kidney** - riñón
difficult - difícil	**liver** - hígado

Notes

Pronunciation: "Estudiando" is the continuous act of studying

Culture: Med school is after high school in most of Latin America

35

What are your hobbies?

¿Cuales son tus pasatiempos?

Cuales - what	tus - your
son - are	pasatiempos - pastimes

Vocabulary

free time - tiempo libre	**expertise** - pericia
interests - intereses	**crafts** - artesanías
likes - gustos	**outdoors** - al aire libre
dislikes - aversiones	**pastures** - pastos
habits - hábitos	**plants** - plantas

Notes

Grammar: "Son" is the third person plural form of "ser," meaning "to be." It is used because "pasatiempos" is plural.

36

I love to read and travel

Me encanta leer y viajar

Me encanta - it enchants me	y - and
leer - to read	viajar - to travel

Vocabulary

adore - adorar	**hiking** - excursiones
drawing - dibujar	**mountains** - montañas
baking - hornear	**wilderness** - yermo
story - historia	**forest** - bosque
flying - volando	**trees** - arboles

Notes

Grammar: "Me encanta" means "it enchants me" but is so commonly meant as "I love/enjoy" that it is understood to mean this.

37

What is your favorite book?

¿Cuál es tu libro favorito?

Cuál - what	libro - book
es - is	favorito - favorite
tu - your	

Vocabulary

literature - literatura	**biography** - biografía
novel - novela	**magazine** - revista
poetry - poesía	**newspaper** - periódico
non-fiction - no ficción	**cartoon** - caricatura

Notes

Grammar: In Spanish, the adjective generally comes after its object in a sentence, resulting in "libro favorito" instead of "favorito libro"

38

My favorite book is "Harry Potter"

Mi libro favorito es "Harry Potter"

Mi - my	es - is
libro - book	"Harry Potter" - name of book
favorito - favorite	

Vocabulary

author - autor	**review** - reseña
poet - poeta	**interesting** - interesante
famous - famoso	**boring** - aburrido
best-seller - el éxito de librería	**well-written** - bien escrito

Notes

Culture: Names stay the same in Spanish but are just pronounced using Spanish pronunciation conventions

39

Where was your last trip?

¿Dónde fue tu último viaje?

Dónde - where
fue - was
tu - your
último - last
viaje - trip

Vocabulary

popular destinations - destinos populares
out of country - fuera del país
travel buddies - compañeros de viaje
atlantic ocean - océano atlántico
pacific ocean - océano pacifico
indian ocean - océano indio
travel agent - agente de viaje
travellers - viajeros
passengers - pasajeros
by sea - en barco

Notes

Grammar: "Fue" is the past tense form of "ir." It is an irregular verb.

40

I visited Mexico last year

Visité México el año pasado

Visité - I visited
el - the
año - year
pasado - last

Vocabulary

survival tips - consejos de supervivencia
human connection - conexión humana
new friendships - nuevas amistades
different cuisine - cocina diferente
exotic food - comida exótica
adventure - aventura
memories - memorias
high standard - alto nivel

Notes

Grammar: Visité is the first person singular past of "visitar". "El" and "pasado" describe año because they are singular and masculine.
Pronunciation: The x in México is pronounced like an h.

First Impression
Primera Impresión

Making a good first impression is important.

Hacer una buena primera impresión es importante.

Always introduce yourself with a smile on your face.

Preséntate siempre con una sonrisa en la cara.

If you meet someone from a different culture, be aware of their cultural sensitivities.

Si te encuentras con alguien de una cultura diferente, ten en cuenta sus sensibilidades culturales.

For example, if you are in South America, people are very passionate about their national soccer teams.

Por ejemplo, si estás en Sudamérica, las personas son muy apasionadas por sus equipos nacionales de fútbol.

You can use such a topic to start a conversation but be careful not to bring up any bad losses or praise the team of a rival country.

Puedes utilizar un tema de este tipo para iniciar una conversación, pero ten cuidado de no mencionar alguna pérdida o alabar al equipo de un país rival.

If you don't know much about a culture, you should stay away from sensitive topics such as politics and religion.

Si no sabes mucho sobre una cultura, debes mantenerte alejado de temas delicados como la política y la religión.

You can always talk about other cultural aspects such

Siempre se puede hablar sobre otros aspectos

as food, language, places to visit, etc.

culturales como la comida, el idioma, los lugares para visitar, etc.

If you mess up in your first meeting, don't be too hard on yourself.

Si te equivocas en tu primera reunión, no seas demasiado duro contigo mismo.

Learn from it and try to do better next time.

Aprende de ello y trata de hacerlo mejor la próxima vez.

Read and Recall Meaning

21. ¿Cómo te llamas?/¿Cuál es tu nombre?

introducción
primer nombre
apellido
apodo
correcta
pronunciación
ortografía
significado

22. Mi nombre es María

mujer
hombre
género
hembra
macho
información
apariencia
personalidad
creencias
religión

23. ¿De dónde eres?

nacionalidad
ciudadano
etnicidad
lugar de nacimiento
nacer
crecer
niñez
educación temprana

24. Soy de Perú

mundo
país
capital
población
bandera
nación
voto
democracia

25. ¿Cuál ciudad en Perú?

pueblo
municipio
sección
barrio
comunidad
experiencias culturales
área
locación
provincia
región
himno

26. Vivo en Lima

vivir
compartir
rentar
poseer
elevador
escaleras
hogar
dos pisos
techo
balcón

27. ¿Cuantos años tienes?

edad
infante
bebé
cambio de pañal
niño
infantil
inmaduro/a
joven
adolescente
legal

28. Tengo veinte años

adulto
viejo
maduro/a
independiente
señor
señora
señorita
mayor
responsabilidad
graduación

29. ¿Qué haces?

emplear
empleo
empleador
empleado
desempleado
trabajo
trabajar
medio tiempo

30. Soy estudiante

ocupación
maestro/a
ingeniero/a
ejército
burócrata
funcionario del gobierno
el no comercial
trabajador social
emprendedor
empresario
educación

31. ¿A qué universidad asistes?

presidente
vicepresidente
profesor asistente
recursos humanos

bien hablado
aprender
enterado
oficinas
decano

32. Asisto a la universidad nacional

admisión
criterios de admisión
oficial de admisión
tamaño de la clase
plazo de solicitud
número uno
inscribir
campus
hostales
departamentos

33. ¿Cuál es tu especialidad?

ciencias políticas
escuela de medicina
licenciatura
maestría
doctorado
investigación
imaginación
arte
ciencias
negocios
ingeniería
humanidades

34. Estoy estudiando medicina

ensayo
luchar
exámenes finales
fácil
difícil
pasar
fallar
cerebro
riñón
hígado

35. ¿Cuales son tus pasatiempos?

tiempo libre
intereses
gustos
aversiones
hábitos
pericia
artesanías
al aire libre
pastos
plantas

36. Me encanta leer y viajar

adorar
dibujar
hornear
historia
volando
excursiones
montañas
yermo

bosque	arboles

37. ¿Cuál es tu libro favorito?

literatura	biografía
novela	revista
poesía	periódico
no ficción	caricatura

38. Mi libro favorito es "Harry Potter"

autor	reseña
poeta	interesante
famoso	aburrido
el éxito de librería	bien escrito

39. ¿Dónde fue tu último viaje?

destinos populares	océano indio
fuera del país	agente de viaje
compañeros de viaje	viajeros
océano atlántico	pasajeros
océano pacifico	en barco

40. Visité México el año pasado

consejos de supervivencia	comida exótica
conexión humana	aventura
nuevas amistades	memorias
cocina diferente	alto nivel

3
Family

"A happy family is but an earlier heaven."

"Una familia feliz no es más que un cielo anterior."

George Bernard Shaw
Irish playwright
(1856 – 1950)

41

My family is from Ecuador

Mi familia es de Ecuador

Mi - my	es - is
familia - family	de - from

Vocabulary

ancestors - antepasados	**tradition** - tradición
family tree - árbol de familia	**values** - valores
family members - miembros de la familia	**customs** - costumbres
kin - pariente	**conservative** - conservador

Notes

Culture: Someone from Ecuador is "ecuatoriano" or "ecuatoriana."

Grammar: "Mi" is possessive because it describes the family, which belongs to the speaker .

42

I have one older brother

Tengo un hermano mayor

Tengo - I have	hermano - brother
un - one	mayor - older

Vocabulary

age gap - diferencia de edad	**compete** - rivalizar
half-brother - medio hermano	**admire** - admirar
twin - gemelo/a	**intelligent** - inteligente
brotherhood - fraternidad	**ignorant** - ignorante
like a brother - como un hermano	**dumb** - tonto/a

Notes

Grammar: Tengo is first person so the "yo" is implied

Pronunciation: The "h" in "hermano" is silent

43

His name is José

Su nombre es José

Su - his	es - is
nombre - name	

Vocabulary

mentor - mentor	**responsible** - responsable
support - apoyo	**serious** - serio/a
gentleman - caballero	**humble** - humilde
good character - buen carácter	**arrogant** - arrogante
role model - modelo a seguir	**stupid** - estúpido/a

Notes

Pronunciation: The j in José is pronounced like an h

Grammar: Su is possessive third person

44

My sister-in-law is from Bolivia

Mi cuñada es de Bolivia

Mi - my	es - is
cuñada - sister-in-law	de - from

Vocabulary

foreigner - extranjero/a	**stranger** - desconocido/a
language barrier - obstáculo lingüístico	**narrow-minded** - limitado/a
cultural differences - diferencias culturales	**liberal** - liberal
common humanity - humanidad común	**Jewish faith** - fe judía
open-minded - libre de prejuicios	**synagogue** - sinagoga

Notes

Grammar: "Mi" is a singular first person possessive article meaning "my." It is neuter, so it can be used to modify a word of any gender.

45

I have one nephew and one niece

Tengo un sobrino y una sobrina

Tengo - I have
un (m)/una (f) - one
sobrino - nephew
y - and
sobrina - niece

Vocabulary

new generation - nueva generación
little ones - pequeños
cute - lindo/a
naughty - travieso/a
noise - ruido
commotion - conmoción
progeny - descendientes
inheritance - herencia

Notes

Grammar: Sobrino/sobrina each require their own article un/una because one is masculine and one is feminine.

46

I also have a younger sister

También tengo una hermana menor

También - also
tengo - I have
una - one
hermana - sister
menor - younger

Vocabulary

pretty - bonito/a
sweet - dulce
loving - cariñoso/a
kind - amable
benevolent - benévolo/a
funny - gracioso/a
humor - humor
feminine - femenina/o
beauty - belleza
shining - brillando

Notes

Pronunciation: The "h" in "hermana" is silent.

47

Her name is Araceli

Su nombre es Araceli

Su - her
nombre - name
es - is

Vocabulary

extrovert - extrovertido/a
talkative - hablador/a
girlfriends - amigas
prank - broma
prankster - bromista
make fun of - burlarse de
quick witted - agudo/a
whistle - silbar
abusive - abusivo/a
inhumane - inhumano/a

Notes

Grammar: "Su" is a third person singular possessive article meaning "his/her". "Sus" is the plural form meaning "their."

48

She recently got married

Se acaba de casar

Se - she
acaba - just finished
de casar - to get married

Vocabulary

marriage ceremony - ceremonia de matrimonio
newly wed - recién casados
wedding dress - vestido de novia
wedding party - fiesta de bodas
priest - sacerdote
wedding - boda
vows - juramentos
married - casado/a

Notes

Grammar: "Se" is different from "ella" because "se" is a reflexive article referring back to "ella." The implied subject of the phrase is "ella," and "se" is equivalent to saying "herself."

49

Her husband lives in Singapore

Su marido vive en Singapur

Su - her	vive - lives
marido - husband	en - in

Vocabulary

abroad - en el extranjero	**challenges** - retos
long distance - a larga distancia	**affection** - afecto
write a letter - escribir una carta	**loyalty** - lealtad
send email - enviar correo electrónico	**call him** - llamarlo

Notes

Culture: "Mi amor," "mi vida," and "cariño" are some common terms of endearment between significant others in Spanish. They mean "my love," "my life," and "dear."

50

My brother-in-law has a big family

Mi cuñado tiene una familia grande

Mi - my	una - a
cuñado - brother-in-law	familia - family
tiene - has	grande - big

Vocabulary

father-in-law - suegro	**son-in-law** - yerno
mother-in-law - suegra	**daughter-in-law** - nuera
middle age - mediana edad	**in-laws** - suegros
respectful - respetuoso/a	**balance** - equilibrio
mutual respect - respeto mutuo	**tribe** - tribu

Notes

Grammar: Adjectives generally come after objects in a sentence.

51

My wife's name is Catalina

Mi esposa se llama Catalina

Mi - my
esposa - wife
se llama - is named

Vocabulary

marital life - vida marital
pregnant - embarazada
fireworks - fuegos artificiales
breastfeeding - amamantamiento
family planning - planificación familiar
argument - pleito
fight - pelear
regret - lamentar
makeup - maquillaje
peace - paz

Notes

Pronunciation: In some places, such as Argentina, the "ll" sound tends to be pronounced slightly like a "j."

52

We have a son and a daughter

Tenemos un hijo y una hija

Tenemos - we have
un (m)/una (f) - one
hijo - son
y - and
hija - daughter

Vocabulary

look alike - parecidos
playground - patio de recreo
play - jugar
swing - columpio
toys - juguetes
duties - deberes
activities - ocupaciones
homework - tarea
mud - lodo
grass - pasto

Notes

Grammar: "Tenemos" is 1st person plural form of "tener" (to have).

53

My father's name is Luís

Mi padre se llama Luís

Mi - my	se llama - is named
padre - father	

Vocabulary

hard life - vida difícil	**impressive** - impresionante
hard-working - trabajador/a	**willpower** - fuerza de voluntad
stoic - estoico/a	**courage** - coraje
expressive - expresivo/a	**honesty** - honestidad
ordinary - ordinario/a	**integrity** - integridad

Notes

Culture: "Padre" is a more formal way to say "father" in Spanish. Most people use "papá" when addressing their dad.

54

My mother's name is Sofía

Mi madre se llama Sofía

Mi - my	se llama - is named
madre - mother	

Vocabulary

motherhood - maternidad	**rights** - derechos
motherly instinct - instinto materno	**obedient** - obediente
unconditional love - amor incondicional	**obedience** - obediencia
high position - posición alta	**joy** - alegría
society - sociedad	**scold** - regañar

Notes

Culture: "Madre" is the more formal way to say "mother," whereas most people say "mamá" to address their mom.

55

My parents love their grandson and granddaughter

Mis padres aman a su nieto y nieta

Mis padres - my parents	nieto - grandson
aman - love	y - and
a su - their	nieta - granddaughter

Vocabulary

strong bond - lazo fuerte	**cuddle** - acariciar
together - juntos	**kiss** - beso
hug - abrazo	**lap** - piernas
cheeks - cachetes	**carry** - cargar

Notes

Grammar: "Nieto" and "nieta" use the same article "su" because it is neuter so it can refer to both masculine and feminine words.

56

My children also love their grandfather and grandmother

Mis hijos también aman a su abuelo y abuela

Mis hijos - my children	a su - their
también - also	abuelo - grandfather
aman - love	y abuela - and grandmother

Vocabulary

laughter - risa	**spoiled** - mimado/a
scream - gritar	**stubborn** - obstinado/a
annoy - fastidiar	**rules** - reglas
feed - dar de comer	**create a mess** - crear un lío

Notes

Grammar: "Su" is used here instead of "sus" because the object of the possessive article in this phrase is singular.

57

I have one uncle and one aunt

Tengo un tío y una tía

Tengo - I have
un (m)/una (f) - one
tío - uncle
y - and
tía - aunt

Vocabulary

wise - sabio/a
wisdom - sabiduría
pragmatic - pragmático/a
anticipate - prever
predict - predecir
signs - señales
prevent - impedir
disaster - desastre

Notes

Pronunciation: The accented "í" in "tío" and "tía" shows that the first syllable of these words is emphasized when you pronounce them.

58

I have one male cousin and one female cousin

Tengo un primo y una prima

Tengo - I have
un (m)/una (f) - one
primo - cousin (m)
y - and
prima - cousin (f)

Vocabulary

extended family - familia extendida
distant relatives - parientes lejanos
barely know them - apenas le conozco
infrequent visits - visitas infrecuentes
quite a while ago - hace bastante tiempo
not close - no cerca
gathering - Reunir
function - función
relatives - parientes

Notes

Pronunciation: "Y" by itself is pronounced "ee."

59

My cousin recently got engaged

Mi primo (m)/prima (f) se acaba de comprometer

Mi - my
primo/prima - cousin (m/f)
se acaba - just finished
de comprometer - to get engaged

Vocabulary

proposal - propuesta de matrimonio
acceptance - aceptación
rejection - rechazo
heart-broken - corazón roto
bride - novia
groom - novio
bridesmaid - dama de honor
best man - padrino de boda

Notes

Grammar: The root verb of "acaba" (third person singular) is "acabar," meaning "to finish."

60

Her fiancé is a doctor

Su novio es médico

Su - her
novio - fiancé/boyfriend
es - is
médico - doctor

Vocabulary

divorced - divorciado/a
widowed - viudo/a
engagement - compromiso
pre-nuptial agreement - acuerdo prenupcial
unmarried - soltero/a
ring - anillo
dowry - dote
jewelry - joyas

Notes

VocExplain: The Spanish word "novio" can mean either "fiancé" or "boyfriend." Spanish word "médico" is a cognate for the English word "medic" i.e. words resemble in appearance and meaning.

Love and Hate
Amor y Odio

As humans, we like to be around people.

Como humanos nos gusta estar cerca de la gente.

This is why family is an important part of our lives.

Es por esto que la familia es una parte importante de nuestras vidas.

Parents are the first caregivers to a child.

Los padres son los primeros cuidadores de un niño.

Strong bonding between a child and parents can build confidence.

La unión fuerte entre un niño y sus padres puede generar confianza.

Having siblings can teach you to compromise and be compassionate, which can help you in your practical life.

Tener hermanos puede enseñarte a comprometerte y ser compasivo, lo que puede ayudarte en tu vida práctica.

For example, my sisters taught me how to bake, and my brothers taught me tennis.

Por ejemplo, mis hermanas me enseñaron a hornear y mis hermanos me enseñaron tenis.

You can also learn and get advice from your grandparents, aunts, and uncles.

También puedes aprender y obtener consejos de tus abuelos, tías y tíos.

Their life experiences can help you make good choices

Sus experiencias de vida pueden ayudarte a tomar

in your own life.

buenas decisiones en tu propia vida.

Cousins can be like your siblings, especially if you are close in age.

Los primos pueden ser como tus hermanos, especialmente si tienen casi tu misma edad.

But on the other hand, sometimes you can get a lot of unsolicited advice.

Pero, por otro lado, a veces puedes obtener muchos consejos no solicitados.

Balance is the key to family ties.

El equilibrio es la clave en los lazos familiares.

In different cultures, family affairs can be handled differently, but the basic idea is to be respectful with your relations.

En diferentes culturas, los asuntos familiares pueden manejarse de manera diferente, pero la idea básica es ser respetuoso con tus relaciones.

Read and Recall Meaning

41. Mi familia es de Ecuador

antepasados
árbol de familia
miembros de la familia
pariente
tradición
valores
costumbres
conservador

42. Tengo un hermano mayor

diferencia de edad
medio hermano
gemelo/a
fraternidad
como un hermano
rivalizar
admirar
inteligente
ignorante
tonto/a

43. Su nombre es José

mentor
apoyo
caballero
buen carácter
modelo a seguir
responsable
serio/a
humilde
arrogante
estúpido/a

44. Mi cuñada es de Bolivia

extranjero/a
obstáculo lingüístico
diferencias culturales
humanidad común
libre de prejuicios
desconocido/a
limitado/a
liberal
fe judía
sinagoga

45. Tengo un sobrino y una sobrina

nueva generación
pequeños
lindo/a
travieso/a
ruido
conmoción
descendientes
herencia

46. También tengo una hermana menor

bonito/a	gracioso/a
dulce	humor
cariñoso/a	femenina/o
amable	belleza
benévolo/a	brillando

47. Su nombre es Araceli

extrovertido/a	burlarse de
hablador/a	agudo/a
amigas	silbar
broma	abusivo/a
bromista	inhumano/a

48. Se acaba de casar

ceremonia de matrimonio	sacerdote
recién casados	boda
vestido de novia	juramentos
fiesta de bodas	casado/a

49. Su marido vive en Singapur

en el extranjero	retos
a larga distancia	afecto
escribir una carta	lealtad
enviar correo electrónico	llamarlo

50. Mi cuñado tiene una familia grande

suegro	yerno
suegra	nuera
mediana edad	suegros
respetuoso/a	equilibrio
respeto mutuo	tribu

51. Mi esposa se llama Catalina

vida marital	planificación familiar
embarazada	pleito
fuegos artificiales	pelear
amamantamiento	lamentar

maquillaje	paz

52. Tenemos un hijo y una hija

parecidos	deberes
patio de recreo	ocupaciones
jugar	tarea
columpio	lodo
juguetes	pasto

53. Mi padre se llama Luís

vida difícil	impresionante
trabajador/a	fuerza de voluntad
estoico/a	coraje
expresivo/a	honestidad
ordinario/a	integridad

54. Mi madre se llama Sofía

maternidad	derechos
instinto materno	obediente
amor incondicional	obediencia
posición alta	alegría
sociedad	regañar

55. Mis padres aman a su nieto y nieta

lazo fuerte	acariciar
juntos	beso
abrazo	piernas
cachetes	cargar

56. Mis hijos también aman a su abuelo y abuela

risa	mimado/a
gritar	obstinado/a
fastidiar	reglas
dar de comer	crear un lío

57. Tengo un tío y una tía

sabio/a	pragmático/a
sabiduría	prever

predecir
señales
impedir
desastre

58. Tengo un primo y una prima

familia extendida
parientes lejanos
apenas le conozco
visitas infrecuentes
hace bastante tiempo
no cerca
Reunir
función
parientes

59. Mi primo (m)/prima (f) se acaba de comprometer

propuesta de matrimonio
aceptación
rechazo
corazón roto
novia
novio
dama de honor
padrino de boda

60. Su novio es médico

divorciado/a
viudo/a
compromiso
acuerdo prenupcial
soltero/a
anillo
dote
joyas

4

Everyday Actions

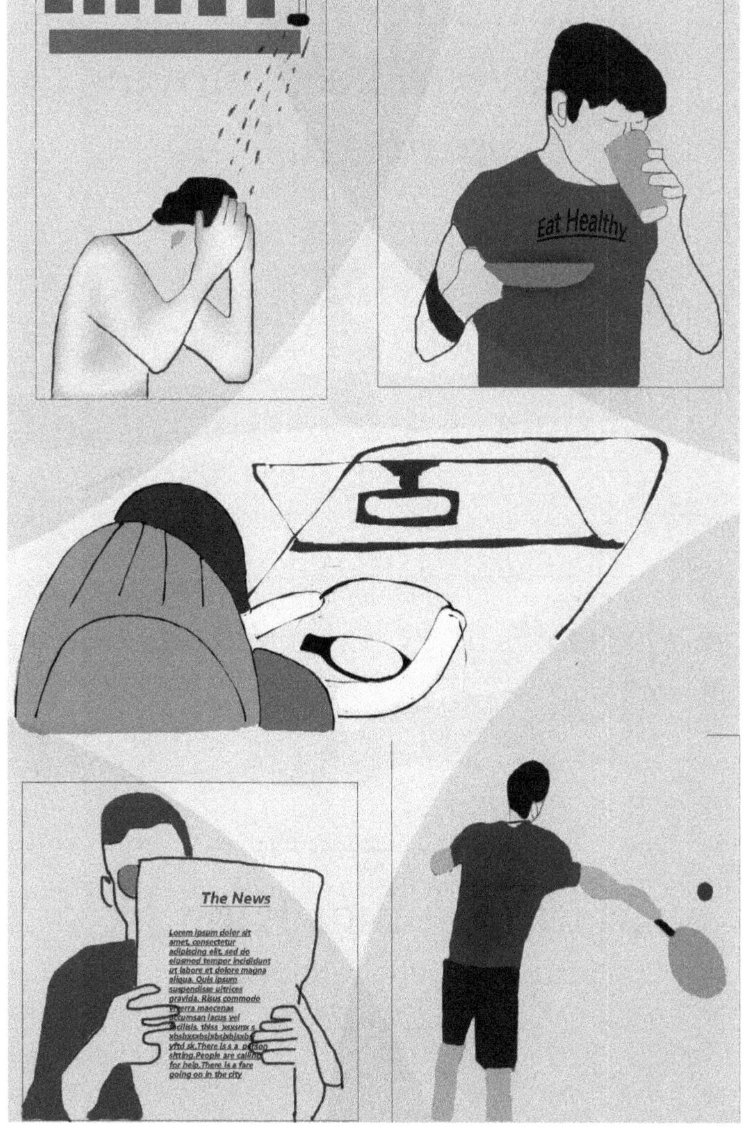

"If you can't fly, then run,
if you can't run, then walk,
if you can't walk, then crawl,
but whatever you do
you have to keep moving
forward."

"Si no puedes volar, entonces
corre,
si no puedes correr, entonces
camina,
si no puedes caminar, gatea,
pero hagas lo que hagas
debes seguir adelante."

Martin Luther King Jr.
American civil rights leader
(1929 – 1968)

61

I wake up at 7 am

Me despierto a las siete de la mañana

Me - I	siete - seven
despierto - wake up	de - of
a las - at	la mañana - the morning

Vocabulary

sleep - dormir	**bedsheet** - sábana
deep sleep - sueño profundo	**pillow** - almohada
bed - cama	**dream** - soñar
make your bed - tender la cama	**alarm** - alarma

Notes

VocExplain: In Spanish, "7 am" translates to "las siete de la mañana," or "the seven (hours) of the morning" in English.

62

I drink a glass of water

Tomo un vaso de agua

Tomo - I drink	de - of
un - a	agua - water
vaso - glass	

Vocabulary

beverage - bebida	**tea** - té
sparkling water - agua carbonada	**bottle** - botella
milk - leche	**refrigerator** - refrigerador
coffee - café	**juice** - jugo

Notes

Grammar: "Agua" is pronounced "ah-wah," instead of "ah-gooah" as one might expect.

63

I brush my teeth

Lavo mis dientes

Lavo - I wash	dientes - teeth
mis - my	

Vocabulary

toothbrush - cepillo de dientes	**dentist** - dentista
toothpaste - pasta de dientes	**mouth** - boca
gums - encías	**tongue** - lengua
floss - hilo dental	**tonsils** - amígdalas

Notes

Grammar: "Lavo" is the first person singular present form of "lavar," which means "to wash." "Mis" is the first person plural form of "mi," which is a possessive article meaning "my."

64

I use the toilet

Utilizo el excusado

Utilizo - I utilize	el excusado - the toilet

Vocabulary

cleanliness - limpieza	**wash** - lavar
toilet paper - papel higiénico	**smell** - olor
wipe - limpiar	**stool** - taburete
flush the toilet - echar agua al excusado	**urine** - orina

Notes

Pronunciation: "Utilizo" is not pronounced with the "u" sound of "utilize" in English, but rather the "u" is pronounced like "oo." Therefore, "utilizo" is pronounced "oo-tee-lee-soh."

65

I take a hot shower

Tomo una ducha caliente

Tomo - I take	ducha - shower
una - a	caliente - hot

Vocabulary

daily routine - rutina cotidiana	**lukewarm water** - agua tibia
shower curtain - cortina de la ducha	**towel** - toalla
water heater - calentador de agua	**exercise** - ejercicio
boiling water - agua hervida	**massage** - masaje

Notes

Grammar: "Ducha" is a feminine word, so the word for "a" translates to "una" since it has a feminine form and "hot" translates to "caliente" which does not have a feminine form since it is neuter.

66

I comb my hair

Peino mi cabello

Peino - I comb	cabello - hair
mi - my	

Vocabulary

hairstyle - peinado	**long hair** - cabello largo
curly hair - cabello rizado	**grey hair** - cabello gris
straight hair - cabello lacio	**hairy** - peludo
short hair - cabello corto	**bald** - calvo

Notes

Grammar: "Peino" is the first person singular and present tense version of "peinar," which means "to comb." From "peinar," the word "peino" derives its meaning of "I comb."

67

I eat my breakfast

Como mi desayuno

Como - I eat
mi - my
desayuno - breakfast

Vocabulary

eggs - huevos
orange juice - jugo de naranja
bread - pan
butter - mantequilla
cheese - queso
omelet - omelet
sausage - salchicha
fruit - fruta
peanuts - cacahuates
almonds - almendras

Notes

Grammar: "Como" is the first person singular present form of "comer," meaning "to eat."

68

I wash my hands

Lavo mis manos

Lavo - I wash
mis - my
manos - hands

Vocabulary

soap - jabón
hand soap - jabón para manos
sink - lavabo
fingers - dedos
thumb - pulgar
nails - uñas
feet - pies
toes - dedos del pie

Notes

Grammar: The word "manos" is the plural form of "mano," which means "hand." Since "manos" is plural, the word "mis" describing it is also plural.

69

I drive to work

Manejo al trabajo

Manejo - I drive
al - to
trabajo - work

Vocabulary

work - trabajo
get off from work - salir del trabajo
hurry up - apúrate
speed limit - límite de velocidad
traffic signal - señal de tráfico
commute - conmutar
car - carro
accelerate - acelerar
overtake - sobrepasar
accident - accidente

Notes

Grammar: "Al" is a contraction of "a el" in Spanish. "A" means "to" and "el" means "the," so together they form "al," meaning "to the."

70

I eat lunch in the café

Almuerzo en el café

Almuerzo - I eat lunch
en - in
el - the
café - café

Vocabulary

eat - comer
drink - beber
bite - mordida
chew - masticar
swallow - tragar
take a sip - sorber
saliva - saliva
jaws - mandíbulas
raisins - pasas
nuts - nueces

Notes

Grammar: "Almuerzo" is the first person singular and present tense of "almorzar," which means "to eat lunch."

71

I pay five dollars for lunch

Pago cinco dólares por el almuerzo

Pago - I pay
cinco - five
dólares - dollars
por - for
el almuerzo - lunch

Vocabulary

lunch - almuerzo
lunch break - descanso para almorzar
natural food - comida natural
light meal - comida ligera
heavy meal - comida pesada
full - satisfecho/a
affordable - asequible
budget - presupuesto
subsidized - subvencionado
paid out - pagado

Notes

VocExplain: "Dollars" is "dólares" in Spanish - it is a cognate.

72

I talk to my boss after lunch

Hablo con mi jefe después del almuerzo

Hablo - I talk
con - with
mi jefe - my boss
después - after
del - the
almuerzo - lunch

Vocabulary

conference room - sala de conferencia
professional - profesional
open and honest - abierto y honesto
talk - hablar
whisper - susurrar
salary - salario
pay - pagar
bonus - extra

Notes

VocExplain: "Con," which means "with," is used instead of "a," which means "to." "Hablo a" implies making a telephone call.

73

I play football in the evening

Juego fútbol en la tarde

Juego - I play	la - the
fútbol - football	tarde - evening
en - in	

Vocabulary

sports - deportes	**game** - juego
team - equipo	**run** - correr
ball - pelota	**jump** - brincar
basketball - baloncesto	**swim** - nadar
play the ball - jugar pelota	**swimming pool** - piscina

Notes

VocExplain: "Fútbol" means "soccer" in the U.S.

74

I cook dinner at 8 pm

Cocino la cena a las ocho de la noche

Cocino - I cook	de - of
la cena - dinner	la - the
a las ocho - at eight	noche - evening/night

Vocabulary

preparation - preparación	**cooking** - cocinar
cut - cortar	**boil** - hervir
slice - rebanar	**stir** - remover
shred - desgarrar	**fry** - freír

Notes

VocExplain: In Spanish, "8 pm" translates to "las ocho de la noche," or "the eight (hours) of the night" in English.

75

I watch a movie

Veo una película

Veo - I watch	película - movie
una - a	

Vocabulary

view - mirar	**comedy** - comedia
action movie - película de acción	**afraid** - asustado
true story - historia verdadera	**nightmares** - pesadillas
horror film - película de terror	**horrible** - horrible

Notes

Grammar: "Veo" is 1st person singular present form of "ver," or "to watch." Other forms of "ver" are "ves" ("you watch"), "ve" ("he/she watches"), "vemos" ("we watch"), "ven" ("you (pl.)/they watch").

76

I read a book

Leo un libro

Leo - I read	libro - book
un - a	

Vocabulary

reviews - críticas	**not available** - no disponible
library - biblioteca	**return** - devolver
borrow - pedir prestado	**bookstore** - librería
available - disponible	**booklet** - libreta

Notes

Grammar: "Leo" is 1st person singular present form of "leer," or "to read." Other forms of "leer" are "lees" ("you read"), "lee"("he/she reads"), "leemos" ("we read") and "leen" ("you (pl.)/they read").

77

I listen to music

Escucho música

Escucho - I listen to	música - music

Vocabulary

music player - reproductor de música	**song** - canción
deeply engrossed - profundamente absorto	**sound** - sonido
classical - clásica	**hear** - escuchar
folk music - música folklórica	**loud** - ruidoso
traditional - tradicional	**speakers** - altavoces

Notes

Culture: Music in Latin America owes its richness to a wide variety of influences from indigenous, African, and European cultures. Some popular styles include mariachi, cumbia, salsa, and bachata.

78

I pray

Yo rezo

Yo - I	rezo - pray

Vocabulary

god - dios	**Christian** - cristiano
prophet - profeta	**Catholic** - católico
saint - santo/a	**Muslim** - musulmán
holy book - libro sagrado	**church** - iglesia
agnostic - agnóstico	**mosque** - mezquita
Buddhism - budismo	**temple** - templo

Notes

Grammar: This phrase can also simply be "rezo" because the "yo" is implied by the first person singular present "rezo."

79

I go shopping on weekends

Voy de compras los fines de semana

Voy - I go
de compras - shopping
los - the
fines - ends
de - of
semana - week

Vocabulary

shopping center - centro comercial
store - tienda
carts - carritos
shopping bag - bolsa de la compra
sale - venta
bargain - ganga
cheap - barato
expensive - caro

Notes

VocExplain: "fin de semana" translates to "end of the week." The plural form for this is "fines de semana" meaning "ends of the week."

80

I like to buy new shoes

Me gusta comprar zapatos nuevos

Me - I
gusta - like
comprar - to buy
nuevos - new
zapatos - shoes

Vocabulary

shoe shop - zapatería
shoe box - caja de zapatos
flip flop - chancla
leather shoes - zapatos de cuero
sandals - sandalias
high heel - tacón alto
laces - cordones
strap - tira
strapped - amarrado/a
stripes - rayas

Notes

Grammar: "To buy" is the infinitive form, so "comprar" is used.

Productive Life
Vida Productiva

The early bird gets the worm.

El primer pájaro se lleva la lombriz.

This saying puts an emphasis on time.

Este dicho pone énfasis en el tiempo.

Being on time can bring balance into your life.

Llegar a tiempo puede traer equilibrio en tu vida.

You can be more productive if you set a routine.

Puedes ser más productivo si estableces una rutina.

For example, if you get up early in the morning, you can take a shower instead of showering late at night.

Por ejemplo, si te levantas temprano en la mañana, puedes tomar una ducha en lugar de ducharte tarde en la noche.

Then you can eat breakfast and get to work on time.

Luego puedes desayunar y llegar a tiempo al trabajo.

Lunch is usually around noon, so make sure you eat healthy and do not spend too much money on it.

Por lo general, el almuerzo es alrededor del mediodía, así que asegúrate de comer sano y no gastar demasiado dinero en él.

When you come home in the evening, you will have free time to do your hobbies.

Cuando vuelvas a casa por la noche, tendrás tiempo libre para hacer tus pasatiempos.

As a general rule to be healthier, eat dinner early, and wait three hours before going to bed.

Como regla general para estar más saludable, cena temprano y espera tres horas antes de irte a la cama.

If you manage your time well, your weekends will also be more productive.

Si manejas bien tu tiempo, tus fines de semana también serán más productivos.

Read and Recall Meaning

61. Me despierto a las siete de la mañana

dormir
sueño profundo
cama
tender la cama
sábana
almohada
soñar
alarma

62. Tomo un vaso de agua

bebida
agua carbonada
leche
café
té
botella
refrigerador
jugo

63. Lavo mis dientes

cepillo de dientes
pasta de dientes
encías
hilo dental
dentista
boca
lengua
amígdalas

64. Utilizo el excusado

limpieza
papel higiénico
limpiar
echar agua al excusado
lavar
olor
taburete
orina

65. Tomo una ducha caliente

rutina cotidiana
cortina de la ducha
calentador de agua
agua hervida
agua tibia
toalla
ejercicio
masaje

66. Peino mi cabello

peinado
cabello rizado

cabello lacio	cabello gris
cabello corto	peludo
cabello largo	calvo

67. Como mi desayuno

huevos	omelet
jugo de naranja	salchicha
pan	fruta
mantequilla	cacahuates
queso	almendras

68. Lavo mis manos

jabón	pulgar
jabón para manos	uñas
lavabo	pies
dedos	dedos del pie

69. Manejo al trabajo

trabajo	conmutar
salir del trabajo	carro
apúrate	acelerar
límite de velocidad	sobrepasar
señal de tráfico	accidente

70. Almuerzo en el café

comer	sorber
beber	saliva
mordida	mandíbulas
masticar	pasas
tragar	nueces

71. Pago cinco dólares por el almuerzo

almuerzo	satisfecho/a
descanso para almorzar	asequible
comida natural	presupuesto
comida ligera	subvencionado
comida pesada	pagado

72. Hablo con mi jefe después del almuerzo

sala de conferencia	susurrar
profesional	salario
abierto y honesto	pagar
hablar	extra

73. Juego fútbol en la tarde

deportes	juego
equipo	correr
pelota	brincar
baloncesto	nadar
jugar pelota	piscina

74. Cocino la cena a las ocho de la noche

preparación	cocinar
cortar	hervir
rebanar	remover
desgarrar	freír

75. Veo una película

mirar	comedia
película de acción	asustado
historia verdadera	pesadillas
película de terror	horrible

76. Leo un libro

críticas	no disponible
biblioteca	devolver
pedir prestado	librería
disponible	libreta

77. Escucho música

reproductor de música	canción
profundamente absorto	sonido
clásica	escuchar
música folklórica	ruidoso
tradicional	altavoces

78. Yo rezo

dios	cristiano
profeta	Católico
santo/a	musulmán
libro sagrado	iglesia
agnóstico	mezquita
budismo	templo

79. Voy de compras los fines de semana

centro comercial	venta
tienda	ganga
carritos	barato
bolsa de la compra	caro

80. Me gusta comprar zapatos nuevos

zapatería	tacón alto
caja de zapatos	cordones
chancla	tira
zapatos de cuero	amarrado/a
sandalias	rayas

5
Everyday Descriptions

"I'm young; I'm handsome; I'm fast. I can't possibly be beat."

"Soy joven; Soy guapo; Soy rápido. No puedo ser vencido."

Muhammad Ali
Heavyweight Boxer
(1942 – 2016)

81

That dog is big

Ese perro es grande

Ese - that	es - is
perro - dog	grande - big

Vocabulary

friendly - amistoso	**bark** - ladrar
well-trained - bien entrenado	**paws** - patas
collar - cuello	**bone** - hueso
leash - correa	**enormous** - enorme
aggressive - agresivo	**wild** - silvestre

Notes

Grammar: "Grande" is a neuter adjective, so it stays the same no matter the gender of its object. Here, it modifies "perro" (masculine).

82

This is a white dog

Este es un perro blanco

Este - this	perro - dog
es - is	blanco - white
un - a	

Vocabulary

animal - animal	**cat** - gato
pet - mascota	**fur** - pelaje
playful - juguetón	**rough** - áspero
attention-seeking - buscando atención	**soft** - suave
loyal - fiel	**horse** - caballo

Notes

Grammar: "Este" means "this" whereas "ese" means "that."

83

He has brown hair

Él tiene el cabello café

Él - he	el cabello - hair
tiene - has	café - brown

Vocabulary

beard - barba	**hairdresser** - peluquero
trim - recortar	**haircut** - corte de pelo
moustache - bigote	**sideburns** - patillas
shave - rasurar	**caress** - acariciar
barber shop - barbería	**blue** - azul

Notes

Grammar: In Spanish, the adjective "café" comes after the object it is describing, "el cabello."

84

That bird is small

Ese pájaro es pequeño

Ese - that	es - is
pájaro - bird	pequeño - small

Vocabulary

duckling - anadón	**fly** - volar
hatch - eclosionar	**air** - aire
newborn - recién nacido	**breathe** - respirar
wings - alas	**lungs** - pulmones
wing-span - envergadura	**landscape** - paisaje

Notes

Pronunciation: The word for "small," "pequeño," contains "ñ." The word "pequeño" is therefore pronounced "pe-KEHN-nee'oh."

85

That is a black bird

Ese es un pájaro negro

Ese - that	pájaro - bird
es - is	negro - black
un - a	

Vocabulary

birds - aves	**goose** - ganso
chicken - pollo	**parrot** - loro
crows - cuervos	**pigeon** - paloma
eagle - águila	**turkey** - pavo

Notes

Grammar: "Pájaro" is a masculine word. Therefore, "un" and "negro" are also masculine to match the gender of "pájaro."

86

She has blue eyes

Ella tiene ojos azules

Ella - she	ojos - eyes
tiene - has	azules - blue

Vocabulary

eyesight problems - problemas de la vista	**pupil** - alumno/a
glasses - gafas	**shrink** - encogimiento
bright - brillante	**expand** - expandir
light - luz	**tears** - lagrimas

Notes

Grammar: "Ojos" is a masculine word, so any word to modify it needs to be masculine or neuter. "Azules" is neuter - it has no gender and can describe masculine or feminine words.

87

My husband is Argentinian

Mi marido es argentino

Mi - my
marido - husband
es - is
argentino - Argentinian

Vocabulary

American - americano
Asian - asiático
British - británico
European - europeo
Indian - indio
Japanese - japonés
Korean - coreano
Turkish - turco

Notes

Script: Note words describing a nationality are not capitalized in Spanish such as "argentino" but the names of countries or places are capitalized because they are proper nouns (e.g. Colombia).

88

He is tall

Él es alto

Él - he
es - is
alto - tall

Vocabulary

physique - físico
height - altura
large - grande
strong body - cuerpo fuerte
ankles - tobillos
calves - pantorrillas
elbow - codo
knees - rodillas
shoulders - hombros
thighs - muslos

Notes

Culture: The average height of a man in Mexico is 5 ft 7.5 inches. The average height of a woman in Mexico is 5 ft 2.5 inches.

89

He is handsome

Él es guapo

Él - he	guapo - handsome
es - is	

Vocabulary

attractive - atractivo	**fat** - gordo
handsome - guapo	**well-dressed** - bien vestido
manly - varonil	**well-groomed** - bien arreglado
muscular - musculoso	**wide chest** - pecho ancho

Notes

Pronunciation: Although "guapo" starts with a g, the word is pronounced "wah-po" because the g is followed by "ua"

90

My wife is Venezuelan

Mi esposa es venezolana

Mi - my	es - is
esposa - wife	venezolana - Venezuelan

Vocabulary

north America - Norteamérica	**middle east** - el medio oriente
south America - Sudamérica	**far east** - lejano este
east Asia - Asia del este	**Africa** - África
west Asia - Asia del oeste	**Europe** - Europa

Notes

Grammar: The Spanish word for "Venezuelan" is "venezolano/a." It can be feminine or masculine, depending on the word it is describing. Since "esposa" is feminine, the feminine form is used.

91

She is short

Ella es baja

Ella - she	baja - short (in stature)
es - is	

Vocabulary

measurements - mediciones	**petite** - chiquita
inches - pulgadas	**weight** - peso
clothing size - talla de ropa	**overweight** - sobrepeso
fitting - ajustado	**underweight** - bajo peso

Notes

VocExplain: The word "baja" means "low" or "short in stature." It is different from "corto/corta," which also means "short" but in terms of length, usually for an object.

92

She is pretty

Ella es bonita

Ella - she	bonita - pretty
es - is	

Vocabulary

beautiful - hermosa	**fair-skinned** - piel blanca
lovely - encantador	**radiant** - radiante
skin - piel	**shiny** - brilloso
dark-skinned - morena	**ugly** - feo

Notes

VocExplain: Words that end in "-ita" or "-ito" are usually diminutive words. Diminutive words imply smallness, cuteness, or endearment. For example, "hijito" means "little son" or "dear son."

93

Your father is old

Tu padre es viejo

Tu - your
padre - father
es - is
viejo - old

Vocabulary

self-reliant - autosuficiente
self-respect - respeto a si mismo
young at heart - joven de corazón
colorful personality - personalidad colorida
elderly - anciano
retired - retirado
caring - cariñoso
thoughtful - atento

Notes

VocExplain: Note the difference between the words "tu" and "tú." The word "tu" is used to denote ownership whereas the word "tú" means "you." The accent on "tú" is useful to distinguish the two.

94

He is weak

Él es débil

Él - he
es - is
débil - weak

Vocabulary

disabled - discapacitado
hard-of-hearing - duro de oído
weak eyesight - mala vista
running nose - nariz que moquea
medical checkup - revisión médica
sick - enfermo
cough - tos
rashes - erupciones
rest - descanso
medicine - medicina

Notes

Pronunciation: The accent on the first syllable of "débil" signifies that this syllable is emphasized so "débil" is pronounced "DEH-beel."

95

He looks sad

Él se ve triste

Él - he
ve - looks
se - himself
triste - sad

Vocabulary

unwell - indispuesto
in pain - adolorido
common ailments - dolencias comunes
malnourished - desnutrido/a
frail - débil
introvert - introvertido
lonely - solitario
complain - quejar

Notes

Grammar: "Se" is a reflexive pronoun meaning "himself." It refers to "el" as the object the verb acts upon. Therefore, "él se ve" means "he looks/appears" because appearance is being done by "he."

96

He is sick

Él está enfermo

Él - he
enfermo - sick
está - is

Vocabulary

illness - enfermedad
diabetes - diabetes
heart patient - paciente del corazón
heart attack - ataque al corazón
surgery - cirugía
acute - agudo
chronic - crónico
arthritis - artritis
dementia - demencia
diarrhea - diarrea

Notes

VocExplain: "Está" means "is" but also signifies a state of being. It is different from "esta," the feminine form of the word for "this."

97

Your mother is young

Tu madre es joven

Tu - your	es - is
madre - mother	joven - young

Vocabulary

elegance - elegancia	**waist line** - cintura
slim - delgado	**energy** - energía
thin - flaco	**youth** - juventud
fresh - fresco	**well-nourished** - bien nutrido

Notes

Talk: "Madre" is used to refer to someone's mother in a more formal, respectful way than "mamá."

98

She is strong

Ella es fuerte

Ella - she	fuerte - strong
es - is	

Vocabulary

natural medicine - medicina natural	**brave** - valiente
traditional medicine - medicina tradicional	**confident** - confidente
acupuncture - acupuntura	**strength** - fuerza
traditional healers - curanderos tradicionales	**coward** - cobarde
healthy eating - alimentación saludable	

Notes

Grammar: "Fuerte" is a neuter word so it can describe both masculine and feminine words

99

She looks happy

Ella se ve feliz

Ella - she
se - herself
ve - looks
feliz - happy

Vocabulary

fortunate - afortunado
lucky - suertudo
long life - larga vida
power - poder
festive mood - actitud festiva
hurt - lastimado
terrible - terrible
vertigo - vértigo
operation - operación

Notes

Talk: "Parece feliz," which means "she appears happy," can also be used. "Parecer" means "to appear."

100

She is healthy

Ella está en buena salud

Ella - she
está - is
en - in
buena - good
salud - health

Vocabulary

healthy - saludable
conscious - consciente
balanced diet - dieta equilibrada
natural diet - dieta natural
nutrients - nutrientes
nutrition - nutrición
fitness - estado físico
home cooked - cocinado en casa

Notes

Grammar: "Está" is used to show a state of being in this sentence. "está en buena salud" signifies "she" is in a state of good health.

Wisdom of the little bird
La sabiduría del pajarito

Sam has a cute little bird who is very clever.

Sam tiene un lindo pajarito que es muy inteligente.

His younger sister Mary has a big fat cat who is always hungry.

Su hermana menor Mary tiene un gato grande y gordo que siempre tiene hambre.

One day, the cat decides to eat the pretty bird.

Un día, el gato decide comerse al pajarito lindo.

She slowly and quietly crawls towards the birdcage.

Ella se arrastra lenta y silenciosamente hacia la jaula del pájaro.

The bird is very intelligent.

El pájaro es muy inteligente.

She can see the cat's reflection in the beautiful picture frame.

Ella puede ver el reflejo del gato en el hermoso marco de imagen.

The bird decides to teach a lesson to the cat.

El pájaro decide enseñar una lección al gato.

When the cat is right under the cage and getting ready to pounce

Cuando el gato está justo debajo de la jaula y preparándose para saltar

The bird loosens the cage screw and flies away.

El pájaro afloja el tornillo de la jaula y se va volando.

The heavy iron cage falls on

La jaula pesada de hierro cae

the cat.

She gets a big bump on her head and angrily meows at the bird.

Mary comes running upon hearing the loud noise.

She scolds the cat for bad behavior.

The wise bird asks Mary to forgive the cat.

On seeing the bird's kindness, the cat apologies to the bird.

They become best friends.

sobre el gato.

Ella sostiene un gran golpe en la cabeza y enojada maúlla al pájaro.

Mary viene corriendo al oír el ruido fuerte.

Ella regaña al gato por portarse mal.

El pájaro sabio pide a Mary que perdone al gato.

Al ver la bondad del pájaro, el gato se disculpa con el pájaro.

Se vuelven mejores amigos.

Read and Recall Meaning

81. Ese perro es grande

amistoso
bien entrenado
cuello
correa
agresivo
ladrar
patas
hueso
enorme
silvestre

82. Este es un perro blanco

animal
mascota
juguetón
buscando atención
fiel
gato
pelaje
áspero
suave
caballo

83. Él tiene el cabello café

barba
recortar
bigote
rasurar
barbería
peluquero
corte de pelo
patillas
acariciar
azul

84. Ese pájaro es pequeño

anadón
eclosionar
recién nacido
alas
envergadura
volar
aire
respirar
pulmones
paisaje

85. Ese es un pájaro negro

aves
pollo
cuervos
águila
ganso
loro

paloma	pavo

86. Ella tiene ojos azules

problemas de la vista	alumno/a
gafas	encogimiento
brillante	expandir
luz	lagrimas

87. Mi marido es argentino

americano	indio
asiático	japonés
británico	coreano
europeo	turco

88. Él es alto

físico	pantorrillas
altura	codo
grande	rodillas
cuerpo fuerte	hombros
tobillos	muslos

89. Él es guapo

atractivo	gordo
guapo	bien vestido
varonil	bien arreglado
musculoso	pecho ancho

90. Mi esposa es venezolana

Norteamérica	el medio oriente
Sudamérica	lejano este
Asia del este	África
Asia del oeste	Europa

91. Ella es baja

mediciones	chiquita
pulgadas	peso
talla de ropa	sobrepeso
ajustado	bajo peso

92. Ella es bonita

hermosa	piel blanca
encantador	radiante
piel	brilloso
morena	feo

93. Tu padre es viejo

autosuficiente	anciano
respeto a si mismo	retirado
joven de corazón	cariñoso
personalidad colorida	atento

94. Él es débil

discapacitado	enfermo
duro de oído	tos
mala vista	erupciones
nariz que moquea	descanso
revisión médica	medicina

95. Él se ve triste

indispuesto	débil
adolorido	introvertido
dolencias comunes	solitario
desnutrido/a	quejar

96. Él está enfermo

enfermedad	agudo
diabetes	crónico
paciente del corazón	artritis
ataque al corazón	demencia
cirugía	diarrea

97. Tu madre es joven

elegancia	cintura
delgado	energía
flaco	juventud
fresco	bien nutrido

98. Ella es fuerte

medicina natural	valiente
medicina tradicional	confidente
acupuntura	fuerza
curanderos tradicionales	cobarde
alimentación saludable	

99. Ella se ve feliz

afortunado	lastimado
suertudo	terrible
larga vida	vértigo
poder	operación
actitud festiva	

100. Ella está en buena salud

saludable	nutrientes
consciente	nutrición
dieta equilibrada	estado físico
dieta natural	cocinado en casa

6
Everyday Things

"Poverty is not made by God, it is created by you and me when we don't share what we have."

"La pobreza no es hecha por Dios, es creada por ti y por mí cuando no compartimos lo que tenemos."

Mother Teresa
Roman Catholic nun
(1910 – 1997)

101

I have a shirt

Tengo una camisa

Tengo - I have
una - a
camisa - shirt

Vocabulary

button - botón
needle - aguja
sewing - cocer
sleeves - mangas
thread - hilo
dress - vestido
sweater - suéter
t-shirt - camiseta
clothing - ropa
size - talla

Notes

Grammar: "Tengo" is the first person singular present form of "tener," meaning "to have."

102

I have a pair of pants

Tengo un par de pantalones

Tengo - I have
un par - a pair
de - of
pantalones - pants

Vocabulary

jeans - pantalones jeans
pajamas - pijamas
shorts - shorts
zipper - cierre
underwear - calzones
bra - sostén
loose - flojo
tight - apretado

Notes

VocExplain: "Par de pantalones," meaning "pair of pants," contains two Spanish cognates for English words. "Par" is a cognate for "pair," while "pantalones" is a cognate for "pants."

103

I have a hat

Tengo un sombrero

Tengo - I have
un - a
sombrero - hat

Vocabulary

cap - gorra
knitted hat - sombrero tejido
straw hat - sombrero de paja
helmet - casco
headscarf - barbijo
scarf - bufanda
gloves - guantes
belt - cinturón

Notes

VocExplain: "Sombrero" is related to the word "sombra," which means shade. A "sombrero" is literally an object that creates shade on your head.

104

I have a pair of shoes

Tengo un par de zapatos

Tengo - I have
un - a
par - pair
de - of
zapatos - shoes

Vocabulary

boots - botas
rain boots - botas de lluvia
sport shoes - zapatos deportivos
socks - calcetines
steps - pasos
stroll - paseo
walk - caminar
limp - cojear

Notes

Pronunciation: The z in "zapatos" is not pronounced like a z in English but rather like an s. "Sah-pah-tos"

105

I have a jacket

Tengo una chamarra

Tengo - I have	chamarra - jacket
una - a	

Vocabulary

coat - abrigo	**raincoat** - impermeable
denim jacket - chaqueta de mezclilla	**windbreaker** - rompevientos
sports jacket - chaqueta deportiva	**hoodie** - capucha
overcoat - sobretodo	**suit** - traje

Notes

Pronunciation: "Chamarra" contains the Spanish "rr" sound. This "rr" sound is pronounced more strongly than a single "r." The resulting pronunciation of "chamarra" is "chah-MAHR-rhah."

106

I have a car

Tengo un carro

Tengo - I have	carro - car
un - a	

Vocabulary

sports car - coche deportivo	**sedan** - sedán
SUV - SUV	**comfortable** - cómodo
truck - camión	**jumpy** - asustadizo
tire - llanta	**brake** - freno
air pressure - presión del aire	**puncture** - perforación

Notes

Pronunciation: The "rr" sound is present again in "carro." Therefore "carro" is pronounced "CAHR-rhoh."

107

I go to school on my bicycle

Voy a la escuela en mi bicicleta

Voy - I go	en - on
a - to	mi - my
la escuela - the school	bicicleta - bicycle

Vocabulary

elementary school - escuela primaria	**uniform** - uniforme
high school - escuela preparatoria	**design** - diseño
kindergarten - el kínder	**motorbike** - moto
middle school - escuela secundaria	**scooter** - escúter
preschoolers - preescolares	**wheel** - rueda

Notes

Talk: "Bicicleta" can also be shortened into "bici"

108

I take a bus to the office

Tomo un autobús a la oficina

Tomo - I take	a - to
un - a	la - the
autobús - bus	oficina - office

Vocabulary

public transportation - transporte público	**route** - ruta
bus station - estación de autobús	**ticket** - boleto
subway - metro	
train - tren	

Notes

Pronunciation: "Autobús" contains an accent on the last syllable of the word, resulting in the pronunciation "au-toh-BOOHS."

109

I have a yellow bag

Tengo una bolsa amarilla

Tengo - I have	bolsa - bag
una - a	amarilla - yellow

Vocabulary

backpack - mochila	**briefcase** - maletín
luxury bag - cartera de lujo	**purse** - cartera
school bag - bolsa escolar	**pocket** - bolsillo
paper bag - bolsa de papel	**wallet** - billetera
plastic bag - bolsa de plástico	**hole** - hueco

Notes

Pronunciation: The word "amarilla" contains the "ll" consonant which produces a sound like the "y" in "yogurt."

110

Can I sit in the chair?

¿Puedo sentarme en la silla?

Puedo - can	en - in
sentarme - I sit	la silla - the chair

Vocabulary

folding chair - silla plegable	**couch** - sofá
stroller - carriola	**cushion** - colchoneta
unlock - abrir cerradura	**wheelchair** - silla de ruedas

child safety seat - asiento de seguridad para niños

Notes

Grammar: "Sentarme" is a reflexive verb containing the reflexive pronoun "me." It means "to seat myself" and is reflexive because the verb "sentar" refers back to the subject performing the action, "me."

111

My phone is on the table

Mi teléfono está en la mesa

Mi - my	en - on
teléfono - phone	la - the
está - is	mesa - table

Vocabulary

electronics - electrónicos	**plug in** - enchufar
phone call - llamada telefónica	**charged** - cargado
low sound - ruido bajo	**turn on** - prender
wire - cable	**turn off** - apagar

Notes

Pronunciation: "Teléfono" contains an accent on its second syllable, resulting in the pronunciation "teh-LEH-foh-noh."

112

Can I use your pen?

¿Puedo utilizar tu pluma?

Puedo - can I	tu - your
utilizar - use	pluma - pen

Vocabulary

ballpoint - bolígrafo	**pencil** - lápiz
fountain pen - pluma fuente	**paper** - papel
fill the form - llenar la forma	**ink** - tinta
notebook - cuaderno	**write** - escribir

Notes

VocExplain: "Pluma" not only means "pen" in Spanish, but it also means "feather." It is also a cognate for the English word "plume," which means "feather" as well.

113

Can you pass me the spoon?

¿Puedes pasarme la cuchara?

Puedes - can you	la - the
pasarme - pass me	cuchara - spoon

Vocabulary

kitchen - cocina	**silverware** - cubiertos
dinner table - mesa del comedor	**kettle** - tetera
fork - tenedor	**pot** - olla
knife - cuchillo	**cupboard** - alacena

Notes

Grammar: "Pasarme" is a reflexive verb meaning "to pass (something) to me." It contains the reflexive pronoun "me," which refers to oneself.

114

Can you pass me the plate?

¿Puedes pasarme el plato?

Puedes - can you	el - the
pasarme - pass me	plato - plate

Vocabulary

give - dar	**glass** - vaso
bowl - bol	**straw** - popote
cup - taza	**salt** - sal
dishwasher - lavador de platos	**pepper** - pimienta

Notes

Grammar: "Puedes" is the second person singular present form of "poder," meaning "to be able to." Other conjugations of "poder" include "puedo" ("I can") and "puede" ("he/she can").

115

The food is delicious

La comida está deliciosa

La - the	está - is
comida - food	deliciosa - delicious

Vocabulary

bland - poco fuerte	**breast piece** - pechuga
salty - salado	**leg piece** - pierna
spicy - picante	**vegetarian** - vegetariano
tasty - sabroso	**whole wheat** - integral
I like it - me gusta	**fried** - freído

Notes

Culture: "Buen provecho" or "provecho" is often said to one before a meal. It is meant to convey the message "enjoy your meal"

116

I need to buy groceries

Necesito comprar los comestibles

Necesito - I need	los - the
comprar - to buy	comestibles - groceries

Vocabulary

broccoli - brócoli	**tomato** - tomate
cucumber - pepino	**vegetables** - verduras
onion - cebolla	**apple** - manzana
potato - papa	**banana** - plátano
spinach - espinaca	**watermelon** - sandía

Notes

Talk: "Necesito ir de compras" is a common phrase understood to mean the same thing

117

I have a dinner reservation at a restaurant

Tengo reservación de cena en un restaurante

Tengo - I have
reservación - reservation
de - for
cena - dinner
en - at
un restaurante - a restaurant

Vocabulary

cancel it - cancélalo
change of plans - cambio de planes
pay cash - pagar con efectivo
pay in credit card - pagar con tarjeta
table - mesa
wait - esperar
main course - plato fuerte
order - pedir

Notes

VocExplain: "Reservación" is a Spanish cognate of "reservation". Their spelling and usage are very similar.

118

I would like to order a soup

Me gustaría pedir una sopa

Me gustaría - I would like
pedir - to ask for
una - a
sopa - soup

Vocabulary

service - servicio
waiter - mesero
appetizer - entrada
bean soup - sopa de frijol
chicken soup - sopa de pollo
fish soup - sopa de pescado
vegetable soup - sopa de verduras
salad - ensalada
fries - papas fritas
baked goods - productos horneados

Notes

VocExplain: Although "ordenar" is a cognate of "order," it can also be meant as "organize," so "pedir" is used here to avoid ambiguity

119

I would like to eat steak

Me gustaría comer un bistec

Me gustaría - I would like
comer - to eat
un - a
bistec - steak

Vocabulary

coal - carbón
iron - plancha
grill - parrilla
slow cooked - cocido a fuego lento
meat - carne
beef - carne de res
lamb - cordero
pork - puerco
chops - chuletas
beef noodle - fideos de res

Notes

Culture: Some of the world's biggest consumers of meat are in Latin America, such as Argentina, Uruguay, and Chile.

120

What would you recommend for dessert?

¿Qué me recomiendas de postre?

Qué - what
me - to me
recomiendas - you recommend
de - for
postre - dessert

Vocabulary

recommend - recomendar
sugar - azúcar
ice cream - helado
jelly - gelatina
taste - probar
sweets - caramelos
sour - agrio
sweet tooth - goloso

Notes

VocExplain: Note the difference between "qué" and "que." "Qué" means "what," whereas "que" means "which."

Blessed Life
Vida Bendita

Life is a series of events.

La vida es una serie de eventos.

Be thankful for your blessings.

Sé agradecido por tus bendiciones.

Do things that bring joy to your life.

Haz cosas que traigan alegría a tu vida.

For example, if you like flowers, how about you start planting them?

Por ejemplo, si te gustan las flores, ¿qué tal si empiezas a plantarlas?

If you like to cook, go and get fresh groceries, prepare your vegetables, and assemble your spices.

Si te gusta cocinar, ve a comprar comestibles frescos, prepara tus vegetales y prepara tus especias.

Sharing also adds positivity to your life.

Compartir también agrega positividad a tu vida.

You can share your laughter with a friend, or you can share your clothes and shoes with someone who is in need.

Puedes compartir tu risa con un amistad o puedes compartir tu ropa y zapatos con alguien que lo necesite.

Giving small gifts to family members can strengthen the relationship.

Dar pequeños regalos a los miembros de tu familia puede fortalecer la relación.

Take pleasure in what you are doing and add a little gratitude to your everyday life.

You have one life, so make the best of it.

Disfruta de lo que estás haciendo y agrega un poco de gratitud a tu vida diaria.

Tienes una vida así que haz de ella lo mejor que puedas.

Read and Recall Meaning

101. Tengo una camisa

botón
aguja
cocer
mangas
hilo
vestido
suéter
camiseta
ropa
talla

102. Tengo un par de pantalones

pantalones jeans
pijamas
shorts
cierre
calzones
sostén
flojo
apretado

103. Tengo un sombrero

gorra
sombrero tejido
sombrero de paja
casco
barbijo
bufanda
guantes
cinturón

104. Tengo un par de zapatos

botas
botas de lluvia
zapatos deportivos
calcetines
pasos
paseo
caminar
cojear

105. Tengo una chamarra

abrigo
chaqueta de mezclilla
chaqueta deportiva
sobretodo
impermeable
rompevientos
capucha
traje

106. Tengo un carro

coche deportivo	sedán
SUV	cómodo
camión	asustadizo
llanta	freno
presión del aire	perforación

107. Voy a la escuela en mi bicicleta

escuela primaria	uniforme
escuela preparatoria	diseño
el kínder	moto
escuela secundaria	escúter
preescolares	rueda

108. Tomo un autobús a la oficina

transporte público	tren
estación de autobús	ruta
metro	boleto

109. Tengo una bolsa amarilla

mochila	maletín
cartera de lujo	cartera
bolsa escolar	bolsillo
bolsa de papel	billetera
bolsa de plástico	hueco

110. ¿Puedo sentarme en la silla?

silla plegable	sofá
carriola	colchoneta
abrir cerradura	silla de ruedas
asiento de seguridad para niños	

111. Mi teléfono está en la mesa

electrónicos	enchufar
llamada telefónica	cargado
ruido bajo	prender
cable	apagar

112. ¿Puedo utilizar tu pluma?

bolígrafo	lápiz
pluma fuente	papel
llenar la forma	tinta
cuaderno	escribir

113. ¿Puedes pasarme la cuchara?

cocina	cubiertos
mesa del comedor	tetera
tenedor	olla
cuchillo	alacena

114. ¿Puedes pasarme el plato?

dar	vaso
bol	popote
taza	sal
lavador de platos	pimienta

115. La comida está deliciosa

poco fuerte	pechuga
salado	pierna
picante	vegetariano
sabroso	integral
me gusta	freído

116. Necesito comprar los comestibles

brócoli	tomate
pepino	verduras
cebolla	manzana
papa	plátano
espinaca	sandía

117. Tengo reservación de cena en un restaurante

cancélalo	mesa
cambio de planes	esperar
pagar con efectivo	plato fuerte
pagar con tarjeta	pedir

118. Me gustaría pedir una sopa

servicio
mesero
entrada
sopa de frijol
sopa de pollo
sopa de pescado
sopa de verduras
ensalada
papas fritas
productos horneados

119. Me gustaría comer un bistec

carbón
plancha
parrilla
cocinado a fuego lento
carne
carne de res
cordero
puerco
chuletas
fideos de res

120. ¿Qué me recomiendas de postre?

recomendar
azúcar
helado
gelatina
probar
caramelos
agrio
goloso

7
Everyday Talk

"People can tell you to keep your mouth shut, but that doesn't stop you from having your own opinion."

"La gente puede decirte que mantengas la boca cerrada, pero eso no te impide tener tu propia opinión."

Anne Frank
Holocaust victim
(1929 – 1945)

121

How is the weather?

¿Cómo está el clima?

Cómo - how	el - the
está - is	clima - weather

Vocabulary

temperature - temperatura	**fall** - otoño
seasons - estaciones	**climate** - clima
spring - primavera	**humidity** - humedad
summer - verano	**tropical** - tropical
winter - invierno	**warm** - cálido

Notes

VocExplain: Note the difference between "cómo" and "como": "cómo" means "how," whereas "como" means "I eat."

122

It is hot

Está caliente

Está - it is	caliente - hot

Vocabulary

sun - sol	**sweat** - sudor
sunny day - día soleado	**soak** - empapar
heat - calor	**drain** - drenar
hot - caluroso	**desert** - desierto
burn - quemar	**sand** - arena
melt - derretir	**swimsuit** - traje de baño

Notes

VocExplain: "It" is implied when you say "está"

123

It is cold

Está frío

Está - it is
frío - cold

Vocabulary

frozen - congelado
hail - granizo
ice - hielo
slippery - resbaloso
snow - nieve
snowfall - nevada
wind - viento
tornado - tornado
flood - inundación
earthquake - terremoto
earth - tierra
nature - naturaleza

Notes

Talk: "Está frío" is used when referring to the weather or atmospheric conditions. "Es frío" is used when referring to an object.

124

It will rain tomorrow

Va a llover mañana

Va - it will
a llover - rain
mañana - tomorrow

Vocabulary

cloud - nube
cloudy - nublado
raining day - día lluvioso
downpour - aguacero
drizzle - llovizna
storm - tormenta
umbrella - paraguas
above the clouds - sobre las nubes

Notes

Pronunciation: "Llover" contains the "ll" sound, resulting in the pronunciation "yoh-VEHR." In addition, "mañana" contains "ñ," resulting in the pronunciation "mahn-NEEAHN-ah."

125

Any plans for the weekend?

¿Tienes planes para el fin de semana?

Tienes - do you have
planes - plans
para - for
el - the
fin - end
de - of
semana - week

Vocabulary

spring break - vacaciones de primavera
summer break - vacaciones de verano
winter break - vacaciones de invierno
go out - salir
park - parque
holiday - feriado

Notes

Grammar: "Tienes" means "you have" when used in a statement, but changes to mean "do you have" when used in a question.

126

I plan to go to the movie theater

Voy al cine

Voy - I will go
al - to the
cine - movie theater

Vocabulary

climbing - trepando
jogging - trotar
hangout - pasar el rato
actor - actor
director - director
movie - película
popcorn - palomitas
singing - cantando
soda - soda
theater - teatro

Notes

Culture: Going to see a movie is a special occasion in much of Latin America

127

I will have a party at my house

Voy a tener una fiesta en mi casa

Voy - I will	en - at
a tener - have	mi - my
una fiesta - a party	casa - house

Vocabulary

celebrate - celebrar	**Christmas** - Navidad
celebration - celebración	**new year** - año nuevo
congratulations - felicidades	**guests** - invitados
thanksgiving - día de acción de gracias	**invitation** - invitación
workers day - día de los trabajadores	**invite** - invitar

Notes

Talk: Another informal way to describe a party is "pachanga"

128

It's my son's birthday

Es el cumpleaños de mi hijo

Es - it is	de - of
el - the	mi - my
cumpleaños - birthday	hijo - son

Vocabulary

gifts - regalos	**to laugh** - reír
balloons - globos	**dance** - bailar
clown - payaso	**sing** - cantar
cake - pastel	**trick** - truco
pineapple - piña	**punishment** - castigo

Notes

Talk: "Cumpleaños" can be shortened to "cumple" for brevity

129

Thanks for the beautiful gift

Gracias por el regalo hermoso

Gracias - thank you
por - for
el - the
regalo - gift
hermoso - beautiful

Vocabulary

thankful - agradecido
headband - diadema
necklace - collar
earrings - aretes
sunglasses - gafas del sol
wristband - pulsera
department stores - tiendas de departamentos

Notes

Pronunciation: "Hermoso" has a silent h, so it is pronounced "er-mo-so"

130

I love you

Te amo

Te - you
amo - I love

Vocabulary

compassion - compasión
to feel - sentir
heart - corazón
heartbeat - latido del corazón
affinity - afinidad
I like you - me gustas
inclination - inclinación
love - amor
sentiments - sentimientos
emulate - emular

Notes

Talk: "Te quiero" can also be used to mean "I love you." The verb "querer" can mean "to want" or "to love."

131

I hate you

Te odio

Te - you odio - I hate

Vocabulary

anger - enojo
disrespect - falta de respeto
out of sight - fuera de vista
show your face - enseñar tu cara
ignore - ignorar
quiet - silencioso
dislike - disgusto
hatred - odio
resent - resentir
resentment - rencor
frustrated - frustrado
vilify - vilipendiar

Notes

Grammar: "Te," unlike "tu" ("you"), is a reflexive article ("yourself") referring back to its second person singular object "tu."

132

I miss you

Te extraño

Te - you extraño - I miss

Vocabulary

cry - llorar
teary - lloroso
good times - buenos tiempos
special moments - momentos especiales
one month old - un mes de edad
separated - separado
attachment - fijación
remember - acordar
forget - olvidar
anniversary - aniversario

Notes

VocExplain: "Extraño" has two meanings in Spanish. It can mean "I miss" or "strange". Beware of ambiguity between the two meanings and make sure to clarify statements with context.

133

I am hungry

Tengo hambre

Tengo - I have	hambre - hunger

Vocabulary

fasting - ayuno	**stomach** - estómago
food - comida	**thirst** - sed
to be full - estar satisfecho	**lips** - labios
drum sticks - patas de pollo	**dry** - seca
dumplings - empanadillas	**wet** - mojado

Notes

Grammar: "Tengo hambre" literally translates to "I have hunger."
VocExplain: Another common way to say "I am hungry" is "estoy hambriento/a"

134

I am tired

Estoy cansado(m)/cansada(f)

Estoy - I am	cansado(m)/cansada(f) - tired

Vocabulary

exhausted - exhausto	**sleepy** - soñoliento
faint - desmayar	**epidemic** - epidemia
unable to walk - incapaz de caminar	**smoking** - de fumar
lack of energy - falta de energía	**consequence** - consecuencia
starving - muriendo de hambre	**seasonal flu** - gripe estacional
sore throat - dolor de garganta	**lung cancer** - cáncer de pulmón

Notes

Talk: "Tengo cansancio" is another way to convey this message. It translates to "I have fatigue"

135

Excuse me

Con permiso/Disculpe

Con - with	Disculpe - forgive/excuse me
permiso - permission	

Vocabulary

allow me - dame permiso	**mistake** - error
manners - modales	**burp** - eructar
please - por favor	**fart** - pedo
no - no	**ginger** - jengibre
yes - sí	**garlic** - ajo

Notes

Talk: "¿Disculpe?" is commonly used to mean "I'm sorry?" if you need someone to repeat themselves

136

I am sorry

Lo siento

Lo - it	siento - I feel

Vocabulary

apology - disculpa	**died** - murió
forgive me - perdóname	**funeral** - velorio
not on purpose - no fue a propósito	**overlook** - pasar por alto
death anniversary - aniversario de muerte	**forgot** - olvidé

Notes

Culture: This is usually used when offering a sincere apology or expression of condolences. It has a formal and intimate connotation.
Talk: "Lo siento mucho" can be used to express stronger lamentation

137

How much is it?

¿Cuanto cuesta?

Cuanto - how much	cuesta - does it cost

Vocabulary

antique - antiguo	**sell** - vender
fake - falso	**auction** - subasta
original - original	**buy** - comprar
made in France - hecho en Francia	**price** - precio
good deal - buena oferta	**money** - dinero

Notes

Culture: Haggling prices can be common in markets throughout Latin America. Many people will make a counter-offer to a stated price.

138

It costs 10 dollars

Cuesta diez dólares

Cuesta - it costs	dólares - dollars
diez - ten	

Vocabulary

cents - centavos	**tip** - propina
coins - monedas	**no way** - de ninguna manera
offer - oferta	**factory price** - precio de fábrica
wasteful spending - gasto inútil	**monthly allowance** - pensión mensual

Notes

Culture: Ecuador, Puerto Rico, Panama, and El Salvador are some Latin American countries that use the American dollar as their currency.

139

What is the time?

¿Cuál es la hora?

Cuál - what	la - the
es - is	hora - hour/time

Vocabulary

early - temprano	**minute** - minuto
late - tarde	**second** - segundo
timely - oportuno	**watch** - reloj de bolsillo
clock - reloj	**airplane** - avión
time - tiempo	**arrival** - llegada
over-stay - permanecer demasiado tiempo	**allowed** - permitido

Notes

Talk: "¿Qué hora es?" is also a common way to say this

140

It is 10:30

Son las diez y media

Son - they are	y - and
las - the	media - a half
diez - ten	

Vocabulary

half-hour - media hora	**on time** - a tiempo
midnight - media noche	**travel** - viajar
quarter to 11 - cuarta para las once	**time zone** - zona horaria
quarter past 10 - diez y cuarto	**unpack** - desempacar
connecting flight - vuelo de conexión	**stop-over** - pernoctar

Notes

Talk: Fractions are used to describe the half and quarter hour.

Keep It Going
Sigue Adelante

Making small talk is an easy way to pass the time.

Hacer una pequeña conversación es una manera fácil de pasar el tiempo.

There are many topics you can talk about.

Hay muchos temas de los que puedes hablar.

You can discuss the weather.

Puedes hablar del clima.

Is it going to be rainy, sunny, or cloudy?

¿Va a estar lluvioso, soleado, o nublado?

Rainy weather makes my grandma very tired and sleepy.

El clima lluvioso hace que mi abuela se sienta muy cansada y con sueño.

Hot weather makes my cat thirsty.

El clima caliente hace que mi gato tenga sed.

You can share what you did over the weekend.

Puedes compartir lo que hiciste durante el fin de semana.

You can ask for suggestions on good food places.

Puedes pedir sugerencias sobre buenos lugares donde comer.

You can complain about the economy and prices.

Puedes quejarte de la economía y los precios.

If nothing else comes to mind, you can always ask a

Si no se te ocurre nada más, siempre puedes preguntar a

person about their future plans.

una persona sobre sus planes futuros.

As you can see, there are many ways to keep a conversation going.

Como puedes ver, hay muchas maneras cómo mantener una conversación.

Read and Recall Meaning

121. ¿Cómo está el clima?

temperatura
estaciones
primavera
verano
invierno
otoño
clima
humedad
tropical
cálido

122. Está caliente

sol
día soleado
calor
caluroso
quemar
derretir
sudor
empapar
drenar
desierto
arena
traje de baño

123. Está frío

congelado
granizo
hielo
resbaloso
nieve
nevada
viento
tornado
inundación
terremoto
tierra
naturaleza

124. Va a llover mañana

nube
nublado
día lluvioso
aguacero
llovizna
tormenta
paraguas
sobre las nubes

125. ¿Tienes planes para el fin de semana?

vacaciones de primavera
vacaciones de verano
vacaciones de invierno
salir

parque	feriado

126. Voy al cine

trepando	película
trotar	palomitas
pasar el rato	cantando
actor	soda
director	teatro

127. Voy a tener una fiesta en mi casa

celebrar	Navidad
celebración	año nuevo
felicidades	invitados
día de acción de gracias	invitación
día de los trabajadores	invitar

128. Es el cumpleaños de mi hijo

regalos	reír
globos	bailar
payaso	cantar
pastel	truco
piña	castigo

129. Gracias por el regalo hermoso

agradecido	aretes
diadema	gafas del sol
collar	pulsera
tiendas de departamentos	

130. Te amo

compasión	me gustas
sentir	inclinación
corazón	amor
latido del corazón	sentimientos
afinidad	emular

131. Te odio

enojo	falta de respeto

fuera de vista	odio
enseñar tu cara	resentir
ignorar	rencor
silencioso	frustrado
disgusto	vilipendiar

132. Te extraño

llorar	separado
lloroso	fijación
buenos tiempos	acordar
momentos especiales	olvidar
un mes de edad	aniversario

133. Tengo hambre

ayuno	estómago
comida	sed
estar satisfecho	labios
patas de pollo	seca
empanadillas	mojado

134. Estoy cansado(m)/cansada(f)

exhausto	soñoliento
desmayar	epidemia
incapaz de caminar	de fumar
falta de energía	consecuencia
muriendo de hambre	gripe estacional
dolor de garganta	cáncer de pulmón

135. Con permiso/Disculpe

dame permiso	error
modales	eructar
por favor	pedo
no	jengibre
sí	ajo

136. Lo siento

disculpa	no fue a propósito
perdóname	aniversario de muerte

murió
velorio
pasar por alto
olvidé

137. ¿Cuanto cuesta?

antiguo
falso
original
hecho en Francia
buena oferta
vender
subasta
comprar
precio
dinero

138. Cuesta diez dólares

centavos
monedas
oferta
gasto inútil
propina
de ninguna manera
precio de fábrica
pensión mensual

139. ¿Cuál es la hora?

temprano
tarde
oportuno
reloj
tiempo
permanecer demasiado tiempo
minuto
segundo
reloj de bolsillo
avión
llegada
permitido

140. Son las diez y media

media hora
media noche
cuarta para las once
diez y cuarto
vuelo de conexión
a tiempo
viajar
zona horaria
desempacar
pernoctar

8
Numbers, Date & Money

"If you're in the luckiest 1% of humanity, you owe it to the rest of humanity to think about the other 99%."

"Si estás en el 1% más afortunado de la humanidad, debes al resto de la humanidad pensar en el otro 99%."

Warren Buffett
CEO of Berkshire Hathaway
(b. 1930)

141

1	uno
2	dos
3	tres
4	cuatro
5	cinco
6	seis
7	siete
8	ocho
9	nueve
10	diez

142

11	once
12	doce
13	trece
14	catorce
15	quince
16	dieciséis
17	diecisiete
18	dieciocho
19	diecinueve
20	veinte

143

21	veintiuno
22	veintidós
23	veintitrés
24	veinticuatro
25	veinticinco
26	veintiséis
27	veintisiete
28	veintiocho
29	veintinueve
30	treinta

144

40	cuarenta
50	cincuenta
60	sesenta
70	setenta
80	ochenta
90	noventa
100	cien
101	ciento uno
105	ciento cinco
110	ciento diez
200	doscientos

145

1000	mil
1250	mil doscientos cincuenta
1500	mil quinientos
1850	mil ochocientos cincuenta
2000	dos mil
million	millón
billion	mil millones

146

First	primero
Second	Segundo
Third	Tercero
Fourth	Cuarto
Fifth	Quinto
Once	Una vez
Twice	Dos veces
Thrice	Tres veces
Four Times	Cuatro veces
Double	Doble
Triple	Triple

147

Today	Hoy
Yesterday	Ayer
Day before Yesterday	Anteayer
Tomorrow	mañana
Day after Tomorrow	Pasado mañana
Monday	lunes
Tuesday	martes
Wednesday	miércoles
Thursday	jueves
Friday	viernes
Saturday	sábado
Sunday	domingo

148

January	enero
February	febrero
March	marzo
April	abril
May	mayo
June	junio
July	julio
August	agosto
September	septiembre
October	octubre
November	noviembre
December	diciembre

149

How do you say bank in Spanish?

¿Cómo se dice "bank" en español?

Cómo - How
se dice - it is said
en español - in Spanish

Vocabulary

speak slowly - habla despacio
can you repeat - puedes repetir
I don't understand - no entiendo
privacy - privacidad
management fee - comisión de gestión
paperwork - papeleo
goals - metas
planning - planear
lend - prestar
lease - arrendamiento

Notes

Grammar: "Spanish" is capitalized but "español" is not. Names of people/places are capitalized in Spanish, but not names of languages.

150

Is there a bank nearby?

¿Hay un banco cerca de aquí?

Hay - is there
un - a
banco - bank
cerca - near
de - to
aquí - here

Vocabulary

business center - centro de negocios
fire station - estación de bomberos
government office - oficina gubernamental
information center - centro de información
police station - estación de policía
post office - oficina postal
investor - inversionista
incentives - incentivos
proximity - proximidad

Notes

Talk: "Por aquí" is also a common way to say "nearby"

151

I want to take out 555 pesos

Quiero sacar quinientos cincuenta y cinco pesos

Quiero - I want
sacar - to take out
quinientos - five hundred
cincuenta - fifty
y cinco - and five
pesos - Mexican currency

Vocabulary

balance - saldo
check - cheque
deposit - deposito
envelop - sobre
funds - fondos
teller - escrutador
withdraw - retirar
long line - fila larga
wait time - tiempo de espera
cashier - cajero

Notes

Culture: Pesos are the official currency of Mexico.

152

I want to change $173

Quiero cambiar ciento setenta y tres dólares

Quiero - I want
cambiar - to change
ciento - one-hundred
setenta - seventy
y tres - and three
dólares - dollars

Vocabulary

currency - moneda
British pound - libra británica
Taiwan dollar - dólar taiwanés
change - cambio
spare change - cambio suelto
request - solicitar
scrutinize - escudriñar
search - buscar

Notes

VocExplain: Just like in English, the word "cambio," or "change," can be used to refer to both money or the action of changing

153

What is the exchange rate?

¿Cuál es el tipo de cambio?

Cuál - what
es - is
el - the
tipo de cambio - exchange rate

Vocabulary

trend - tendencia
market fluctuate - fluctuación del mercado
monetary policy - política monetaria
economics - ciencias económicas
demand - demanda
supply - suministro
import - importar
export - exportar
verify - verificar
cheating - trampa

Notes

Culture: The American dollar tends to go a long way in many Latin American countries.

154

It is 6.92

Es del seis punto nueve dos

Es - it is
del - of the
seis - six
punto - point
nueve - nine
dos - two

Vocabulary

compare - comparar
ratio - proporción
calculate - calcular
add - sumar
divide - dividir
fraction - fracción
multiply - multiplicar
subtract - restar
less - menos
more - más

Notes

Culture: In Spain, a comma is used to denote a decimal point.

155

What is the price of this jacket?

¿Cuanto cuesta esta chamarra?

Cuanto - how much
cuesta - costs
esta - this
chamarra - jacket

Vocabulary

material - material
single layered - una sola capa
thick - grueso
double layered - doble capa
cotton - algodón
leather - cuero
polyester - poliéster
wool - lana

Notes

Culture: "Chaqueta" is a common word for jacket in many Latin American countries. Just don't say it in Mexico unless you want stares and chuckles.

156

It costs 58 pesos

Cuesta cincuenta y ocho pesos

Cuesta - it costs
cincuenta y ocho - fifty-eight
pesos - Mexican currency

Vocabulary

discount - descuento
transaction - transacción
savings - ahorros
rich - rico
poor - pobre
quality - calidad
luxury - lujo
modern - moderno
posh - elegante
upscale - de lujo

Notes

VocExplain: Numbers like "fifty-eight" in Spanish are written or spoken using "y" instead of a hyphen, hence "cincuenta y ocho"

157

Do you have something cheaper?

¿Tienes algo más barato?

Tienes - do you have	más - more
algo - something	barato - cheap

Vocabulary

bother - molestar	**advantage** - ventaja
discuss - discutir	**disadvantage** - desventaja
haggle - regatear	**economical** - económico
irritate - irritar	**half-price** - medio precio
negotiate - negociar	**competition** - competencia

Notes

Culture: It is not uncommon to bargain for prices and ask for a lower price

158

Yes. This one costs 47 pesos.

Sí. Este cuesta cuarenta y siete pesos.

Sí - yes	cuarenta y siete - forty-seven
este - this one	pesos - Mexican currency
cuesta - costs	

Vocabulary

greedy - codicioso	**donations** - donaciones
generous - generoso	**charitable** - caritativo
prosperity - prosperidad	**wealth** - riqueza
shrewd - perspicaz	

Notes

Culture: Sometimes products at small shops or markets in Latin America do not have prices marked so you have to ask for the price

159

I will pay with credit card

Voy a pagar con tarjeta de crédito

Voy - I will	con - with
a - to	tarjeta de crédito - credit card
pagar - pay	

Vocabulary

credit card - tarjeta de crédito	**contract** - contrato
debit card - tarjeta de débito	**deduct** - deducir
interest rate - tasa de interés	**expenses** - gastos
loan - préstamo	**insurance** - seguro
prepaid card - tarjeta de prepago	**payment** - pago

Notes

Culture: In Latin America, it is common to pay with cash.

160

There is a 2% fee for foreign cards

Hay una cuota del dos por ciento para tarjetas extranjeras

Hay - there is	por ciento - percent
una cuota - a fee	para - for
del - of	tarjetas - cards
dos - two	extranjeras - foreign

Vocabulary

extra charge - carga extra	**illegal** - ilegal
late fee - cargo por demora	**theft** - robo
penalty - penalización	**sales tax** - impuesto de venta
unfair - injusto	**opportunist** - oportunista

Notes

Grammar: "Cuota" is a cognate of the English word "quota."

More With Less
Más Con Menos

Whenever you travel, you should be conscious of money.

Cada vez que viajes, debes ser consciente del dinero.

If you know how to navigate within your budget, you will be fine.

Si sabes cómo navegar dentro de tu presupuesto, estarás bien.

You should know how to calculate the exchange rate.

Debes saber cómo calcular el tipo de cambio.

Rather than going to expensive tourist places, ask the locals where they shop.

En lugar de ir a lugares turísticos caros, pregunta a los locales dónde van de compras.

Better yet, if you have a local friend, go shopping with her.

Mejor aún, si tienes una amiga local, ve de compras con ella.

She can take you to the markets with the best prices.

Ella puede llevarte a los mercados con los mejores precios.

She can further save you money by negotiating with the shopkeeper.

Ella puede ahorrarte dinero negociando con el comerciante.

Once my friend and I were trying to buy the same jacket.

Una vez mi amiga y yo intentábamos comprar la misma chamarra.

She went to a big department store and bought it for 25$.

Ella fue a una tienda grande y la compró por $25.

I asked a friend of mine who works in retail to help me find a good deal.

Pregunté a una amiga mía que trabaja en el comercio que me ayude a encontrar un buen negocio.

She advised me to go to a different store in another part of the city.

Ella me aconsejó que fuera a otra tienda en otra parte de la ciudad.

I followed her advice and ended up buying the same jacket for $12.

Seguí su consejo y terminé comprando la misma chamarra por $12.

Read and Recall Meaning

141. Numbers 1 - 10

uno
dos
tres
cuatro
cinco
seis
siete
ocho
nueve
diez

142. Numbers 11 - 20

once
doce
trece
catorce
quince
dieciséis
diecisiete
dieciocho
diecinueve
veinte

143. Numbers 21 - 30

veintiuno
veintidós
veintitrés
veinticuatro
veinticinco
veintiséis
veintisiete
veintiocho
veintinueve
treinta

144. Numbers between 40 and 200

cuarenta
cincuenta
sesenta
setenta
ochenta
noventa
cien
ciento uno
ciento cinco
ciento diez
doscientos

145. Big Numbers

mil
mil doscientos cincuenta
mil quinientos
mil ochocientos cincuenta

dos mil
millón
mil millones

146. Ordinals

primero
Segundo
Tercero
Cuarto
Quinto
Una vez
Dos veces
Tres veces
Cuatro veces
Doble
Triple

147. Days

Hoy
Ayer
Anteayer
mañana
Pasado mañana
lunes
martes
miércoles
jueves
viernes
sábado
domingo

148. Months

enero
febrero
marzo
abril
mayo
junio
julio
agosto
septiembre
octubre
noviembre
diciembre

149. ¿Cómo se dice "bank" en español?

habla despacio
puedes repetir
no entiendo
privacidad
comisión de gestión
papeleo
metas
planear
prestar
arrendamiento

150. ¿Hay un banco cerca de aquí?

centro de negocios
estación de bomberos
oficina gubernamental
centro de información
estación de policía
oficina postal

inversionista
incentivos
proximidad

151. Quiero sacar quinientos cincuenta y cinco pesos

saldo
cheque
deposito
sobre
fondos
escrutador
retirar
fila larga
tiempo de espera
cajero

152. Quiero cambiar ciento setenta y tres dólares

moneda
libra británica
dólar taiwanés
cambio
cambio suelto
solicitar
escudriñar
buscar

153. ¿Cuál es el tipo de cambio?

tendencia
fluctuación del mercado
política monetaria
ciencias económicas
demanda
suministro
importar
exportar
verificar
trampa

154. Es del seis punto nueve dos

comparar
proporción
calcular
sumar
dividir
fracción
multiplicar
restar
menos
más

155. ¿Cuanto cuesta esta chamarra?

material
una sola capa
grueso
doble capa
algodón
cuero
poliéster
lana

156. Cuesta cincuenta y ocho pesos

descuento
transacción

ahorros
rico
pobre
calidad

lujo
moderno
elegante
de lujo

157. ¿Tienes algo más barato?

molestar
discutir
regatear
irritar
negociar

ventaja
desventaja
económico
medio precio
competencia

158. Sí. Este cuesta cuarenta y siete pesos.

codicioso
generoso
prosperidad
perspicaz

donaciones
caritativo
riqueza

159. Voy a pagar con tarjeta de crédito

tarjeta de crédito
tarjeta de débito
tasa de interés
préstamo
tarjeta de prepago

contrato
deducir
gastos
seguro
pago

160. Hay una cuota del dos por ciento para tarjetas extranjeras

carga extra
cargo por demora
penalización
injusto

ilegal
robo
impuesto de venta
oportunista

9
Vacations

"Traveling - it leaves you speechless, then turns you into a storyteller."

"Viajar - te deja sin palabras, luego te convierte en un cuentacuentos."

Ibn Battuta

World Traveller from Morocco

(1304 – 1369)

161

We are going to Buenos Aires next week

Nosotros vamos a Buenos Aires la próxima semana

Nosotros - we
vamos - are going
a - to
la - the
próxima - next
semana - week

Vocabulary

destination - destino
work related - relacionado al trabajo
passport - pasaporte
alone - solitario/a
with family - con familia
never before - nunca antes
first-time - primera vez
once before - una vez antes

Notes

Talk: The "nosotros" is optional in this sentence since it is implied by the first-person plural tense of "vamos"

162

Is it a direct flight?

¿Es un vuelo directo?

Es - is it
un - a
vuelo - flight
directo - direct

Vocabulary

id card - tarjeta de identificación
security check - revisión de seguridad
empty pockets - bolsillos vacíos
collect my things - recoger mis cosas
last minute sale - venta de última hora
scanning machine - maquina de escaneo
liquids - líquidos
airport - aeropuerto
pat down - palmadita
road trip - **viaje en carretera**
boarding gate - puerta de abordaje
overnight flight - vuelo nocturno

Notes

VocExplain: "Directo" is a cognate of the English word "direct"

163

Yes. We were lucky to get cheap tickets.

Sí. Tuvimos suerte en conseguir boletos baratos.

Sí - yes	en conseguir - in obtaining
tuvimos - we had	boletos - tickets
suerte - luck	baratos - cheap

Vocabulary

back seats - asientos traseros	**take off** - despegar
front seats - asientos delanteros	**awesome** - chido
aisle seat - asiento de pasillo	**luck** - suerte
leg room - espacio para las pierna	**unbelievable** - increíble
window seat - asiento de la ventana	**unlucky** - desafortunado

Notes

Talk: "Fuimos suertudos" can also be used to mean "we were lucky"

164

I need help

Necesito ayuda

Necesito - I need	ayuda - help

Vocabulary

need - necesidad	**flight attendant** - aeromozo
emergency - emergencia	**flight status** - estado del vuelo
ambulance - ambulancia	**help** - ayuda
lost and found - objetos perdidos	**problem** - problema
connecting flight - vuelo de conexión	**suffering** - sufrimiento
first-aid station - estación de primeros auxilios	**unhappy** - infeliz

Notes

Talk: The imperative form of this statement is "ayúdame" or "help me"

165

I lost my luggage

Perdí mis maletas

Perdí - I lost
mis - my
maletas - luggage

Vocabulary

duty free - libre de impuestos
gift shop - tienda de regalos
overweight - sobrepeso
underweight - bajo peso
weight limit - límite de peso
carry-on - bolso de mano
key - llave
open it - ábrelo
close it - ciérralo
delicate things - cosas delicadas

Notes

Grammar: "Perdí" is the first person singular past tense form of "perder," which means "to lose"

166

One bag is red and the other is orange

Una maleta es roja y la otra es anaranjada

Una maleta - one bag
es - is
roja - red
y - and
la otra - the other
anaranjada - orange

Vocabulary

color - color
black - negro
golden - dorado
green - verde
orange - anaranjado
pink - rosado
purple - morado
silver - plateado
white - blanco
yellow - amarillo

Notes

Grammar: "Maleta" is feminine so "una," "roja," and "otra" are too.

167

I need to go to the hotel

Necesito ir al hotel

Necesito - I need
ir - to go
al - to the
hotel - hotel

Vocabulary

official taxi - taxi oficial
car registration - registración de auto
fuel station - gasolinera
fill the tank - llenar el tanque
fuel indicator - indicador de combustible
number plate - numero de placas
share the ride - compartir el viaje
rent a car - rentar auto
safety - seguridad
scam - estafa

Notes

Talk: "Tengo que ir" can also be used in place of "necesito ir" and it means "I have to go".

168

Do you have the hotel address?

¿Tienes la dirección del hotel?

Tienes - do you have
la - the
dirección - address
del - of the
hotel - hotel

Vocabulary

road - carretera
street - calle
city center - centro de ciudad
road work - trabajo en la carretera
bumpy ride - paseo lleno de baches
go fast - ir rápido
rush hour - hora pico
traffic - tráfico
danger - peligro
slow down - reducir velocidad

Notes

Culture: The way streets are set up in Latin America varies a lot.

169

How much is the cab fare?

¿Cuanto cuesta la tarifa del taxi?

Cuanto - how much	tarifa - fare
cuesta - costs	del - of the
la - the	taxi - taxi

Vocabulary

reset meter - reiniciar el motor	**cab driver** - taxista
over charge - sobre carga	**cab fare** - tarifa de taxi
useful tips - consejos útiles	**how far?** - qué lejos
city tour - paseo por la ciudad	**how long?** - cuanto tiempo

Notes

Culture: Taxis are very common in large urban areas of Latin America. They are everywhere on the streets.

170

Can I have the receipt?

¿Puedo tener el recibo?

Puedo - can I	el - the
tener - have	recibo - receipt

Vocabulary

very good - muy bueno	**waiting** - esperando
not good - no bueno	**engaging** - cautivador
outside the gate - fuera de la puerta	**navigate** - navegar
entrance fee - precio de la entrada	**invoice** - factura
highway fee - tarifa de carretera	**parking** - estacionamiento
turn - virar	**stop** - detener

Notes

Grammar: "Tener" is an infinitive verb meaning "to have"

171

I have a room reservation

Tengo una reservación de habitación

Tengo - I have	de - of
una - a	habitación - room
reservación	

Vocabulary

booking - reserva	**bedroom** - habitación
lounge - salón	**single bed** - cama individual
availability - disponibilidad	**double bed** - cama doble
top floor - ultimo piso	**separate beds** - camas separadas
ground floor - planta baja	**mattress** - colchón

Notes

VocExplain: "Habitación" has the same root as the word "habitat"

172

What is the check out time?

¿Cuál es el tiempo de salida?

Cuál - what	tiempo - time
es - is	de - of
el - the	salida - exit

Vocabulary

busy season - temporada ocupada	**complimentary** - complementario
internet fee - tarifa de internet	**room service** - servicio de cuarto
laundry - lavandería	**room charges** - cargas de habitación
drop-off service - servicio de entrega	**return the keys** - devolver las llaves

Notes

VocExplain: "La hora de salida" can also be used in place of "el tiempo de salida"

173

Is there a market here?

¿Hay un mercado aquí?

Hay - is there	mercado - market
un - a	aquí - here

Vocabulary

farmer's market - mercado de agricultores
specialty shops - tiendas de especialidad
night market - mercado nocturno
supermarket - supermercado
traditional stores - tiendas tradicionales

Notes

Culture: Open-air markets are very common in Latin America. You can find a variety of things from fresh produce to handmade clothing.

174

Go straight, take a right and then a left

Ve derecho, toma una derecha y luego una izquierda

Ve - go	una derecha - a right
derecho - straight	y luego - and then
toma - take	una izquierda - a left

Vocabulary

directions - direcciones	**beneath** - debajo
above - encima	**besides** - además
behind - detrás	**down** - abajo
below - bajo	**up** - arriba

Notes

VocExplain: Be careful not to confuse "derecho," meaning to go straight, and "derecha," which means to go right.

175

Can you recommend good places to visit?

¿Puedes recomendar buenos lugares para visitar?

Puedes - can you	lugares - places
recomendar - recommend	para - for
buenos - good	visitar - to visit

Vocabulary

discover - descubrir	**ocean** - océano
tourism - turismo	**beach** - playa
tourists - turistas	**river** - río
attractions - atracciones	**lake** - lago

Notes

Grammar: "Buenos" is masculine and plural to match the masculine plural "lugares"

176

There are a lot of museums near the city center

Hay muchos museos cerca del centro

Hay - there are	cerca - near
muchos - many	del - to the
museos - museums	centro - city center

Vocabulary

historic sites - sitios históricos	**architecture** - arquitectura
monuments - monumentos	**European touch** - toque europeo
old town - pueblo viejo	**Asian influence** - influencia asiática
buildings - edificios	**cultural festivals** - ferias culturales

Notes

Culture: Many cities and towns in Latin America have a "centro," or city center square, a legacy of Spanish colonial times.

177

Are there good restaurants nearby?

¿Hay buenos restaurantes por aquí?

Hay - are there
buenos - good
restaurantes - restaurants
por - by
aquí - here

Vocabulary

eating out - comer afuera
to eat - comer
unpopular - impopular
under-cooked - medio crudo
bakery - panadería
candy shop - tienda de dulces
secret recipe - receta secreta
raw vegetables - verduras crudas

Notes

Grammar: "Buenos" is masculine and plural to match the masculine plural "restaurantes"

178

Can you bring the check/bill please?

¿Puedes traer la cuenta por favor?

Puedes - can you
traer - bring
la - the
cuenta - check/bill
por favor - please

Vocabulary

restaurant - restaurante
leftovers - sobras
trash - desperdicio
great service - servicio genial
value added tax - impuesto al valor agregado
service fee - tarifa de servicio
waste bin - canasta de basura
checkout - salida
light food - comida ligera
menu - menú

Notes

Grammar: "Traer" is the infinitive verb meaning "to bring"

179

Can you take my photo?

¿Me puedes tomar una foto?

Me - of me	tomar - take
puedes - can you	una foto - a photo

Vocabulary

camera - cámara	**maybe** - quizás
memory - memoria	**want to** - querer
scenery - escenario	**need to** - necesitar
family portrait - retrato familiar	**have to** - tener que
wedding photo - foto de boda	**hold it** - tenerlo

Notes

VocExplain: "Tomar" means "to take but it can also mean "to drink." Be careful not to confuse the two meanings.

180

I need to see a doctor

Necesito ver un médico

Necesito - I need	un - a
ver - to see	médico - doctor

Vocabulary

ill - mal	**nurse** - enfermera
injured - lesionado	**out of breath** - sin aliento
hospital - hospital	**pulse** - pulso
clinic - clínica	**treatment** - tratamiento
doctor - doctor	**blood** - sangre
eating disorder - desorden alimenticio	**organs** - órganos

Notes

VocExplain: "Médico" is a cognate of the English word "medic"

Best Time Of The Year
El Mejor Tiempo Del Año

I take a vacation once a year.

Tomo vacaciones una vez al año.

This is the best time of the year, although getting ready for it can be overwhelming.

Esta es la mejor época del año, aunque prepararse para ella puede ser abrumador.

You have to get tickets if you are traveling by air, bus, or train.

Tienes que conseguir boletos si viajas en avión, autobús o tren.

Managing your luggage by packing light is a good idea.

Manejar su equipaje al empacar ligeramente es una buena idea.

My daughter went to Turkey for a month.

Mi hija fue a Turquía por un mes.

She lost her bag, but luckily someone found it and returned it to her.

Perdió su bolso, pero afortunadamente alguien lo encontró y se lo devolvió.

She then took a cab from the airport to her hotel.

Luego ella tomó un taxi desde el aeropuerto hasta su hotel.

The hotel was near the city center so she could explore the city on foot.

El hotel estaba cerca del centro de la ciudad para que ella pudiera explorar la ciudad a pie.

She loves to try new cuisines. She tried a different dish every day.

A ella le encanta probar nuevas cocinas. Ella probó un plato diferente cada día.

She really enjoyed seeing all the historical places in Turkey.

Ella verdaderamente disfrutó ver todos los lugares históricos en Turquía.

This included old mosques, churches, and palaces.

Esto incluía mezquitas antiguas, iglesias, y palacios.

You don't always have to go to a far-away place to enjoy your vacations.

No siempre tienes que ir a un lugar lejano para disfrutar de tus vacaciones.

Exploring your own city on foot can reveal new secrets and connect you to the city in new ways.

Explorar tu propia ciudad a pie puede revelar nuevos secretos y conectarte con la ciudad en nuevas maneras.

I tried this last summer, and it was a great adventure. I would recommend you try that on your next vacation.

Lo intenté el verano pasado y fue una gran aventura. Te recomendaría que lo intentes en tus próximas vacaciones.

Read and Recall Meaning

161. Nosotros vamos a Buenos Aires la próxima semana

destino	con familia
relacionado al trabajo	nunca antes
pasaporte	primera vez
solitario/a	una vez antes

162. ¿Es un vuelo directo?

tarjeta de identificación	líquidos
revisión de seguridad	aeropuerto
bolsillos vacíos	palmadita
recoger mis cosas	viaje en carretera
venta de última hora	puerta de abordaje
maquina de escaneo	vuelo nocturno

163. Sí. Tuvimos suerte en conseguir boletos baratos.

asientos traseros	despegar
asientos delanteros	chido
asiento de pasillo	suerte
espacio para las pierna	increíble
asiento de la ventana	desafortunado

164. Necesito ayuda

necesidad	aeromozo
emergencia	estado del vuelo
ambulancia	ayuda
objetos perdidos	problema
vuelo de conexión	sufrimiento
estación de primeros auxilios	infeliz

165. Perdí mis maletas

libre de impuestos	sobrepeso
tienda de recuerdos	bajo peso

límite de peso
bolso de mano
llave
ábrelo
ciérralo
cosas delicadas

166. Una maleta es roja y la otra es anaranjada

color
negro
dorado
verde
anaranjado
rosado
morado
plateado
blanco
amarillo

167. Necesito ir al hotel

taxi oficial
registración de auto
gasolinera
llenar el tanque
indicador de combustible
numero de placas
compartir el viaje
rentar auto
seguridad
estafa

168. ¿Tienes la dirección del hotel?

carretera
calle
centro de ciudad
trabajo en la carretera
paseo lleno de baches
ir rápido
hora pico
tráfico
peligro
reducir velocidad

169. ¿Cuanto cuesta la tarifa del taxi?

reiniciar el motor
sobre carga
consejos útiles
paseo por la ciudad
taxista
tarifa de taxi
qué lejos
cuanto tiempo

170. ¿Puedo tener el recibo?

muy bueno
no bueno
fuera de la puerta
precio de la entrada
tarifa de carretera
virar
esperando
cautivador
navegar
factura
estacionamiento
detener

171. Tengo una reservación de habitación

reserva
salón
disponibilidad
ultimo piso
planta baja
habitación
cama individual
cama doble
camas separadas
colchón

172. ¿Cuál es el tiempo de salida?

temporada ocupada
tarifa de internet
lavandería
servicio de entrega
complementario
servicio de cuarto
cargas de habitación
devolver las llaves

173. ¿Hay un mercado aquí?

mercado de agricultores
tiendas de especialidad
mercado nocturno
supermercado
tiendas tradicionales

174. Ve derecho, toma una derecha y luego una izquierda

direcciones
encima
detrás
bajo
debajo
además
abajo
arriba

175. ¿Puedes recomendar buenos lugares para visitar?

descubrir
turismo
turistas
atracciones
océano
playa
río
lago

176. Hay muchos museos cerca del centro

sitios históricos
monumentos
pueblo viejo
edificios
arquitectura
toque europeo
influencia asiática
ferias culturales

177. ¿Hay buenos restaurantes por aquí?

comer afuera
comer
impopular
medio crudo
panadería
tienda de dulces
receta secreta
verduras crudas

178. ¿Puedes traer la cuenta por favor?

restaurante
sobras
desperdicio
servicio genial
impuesto al valor agregado
tarifa de servicio
canasta de basura
salida
comida ligera
menú

179. ¿Me puedes tomar una foto?

cámara
memoria
escenario
retrato familiar
foto de boda
quizás
querer
necesitar
tener que
tenerlo

180. Necesito ver un médico

mal
lesionado
hospital
clínica
doctor
desorden alimenticio
enfermera
sin aliento
pulso
tratamiento
sangre
órganos

10
Socialize

"A man is known by the company he keeps."

"Un hombre es conocido por la compañía que mantiene."

Aesop

Greek storyteller

(620 – 564 BCE)

Hey friend. Where have you been?

Hola amigo(m)/amiga(f). ¿En dónde has estado?

Hola - hello
amigo(m)/amiga(f) - friend
en dónde - where
has - have you
estado - been

Vocabulary

friendship - amistad
besties - mejores amigos
childhood friend - amigo de la niñez
long-lasting - duradero
short-lived - corta vida
reunion - reunión
enemy - enemigo
opponent - adversario

Notes

Grammar: In English, "friend" has no gender but in Spanish it can be masculine or feminine based on the gender of the person.

182

I have been busy with work

He estado ocupado(m)/ocupada(f) con el trabajo

He - I have
estado - been
ocupado(m)/ocupada(f) - busy
con - with
el - the
trabajo - work

Vocabulary

busy - ocupado
pressure - presión
stress - estrés
political analyst - analista político
elections - elecciones
popular opinion - opinión popular
socialism - socialismo
communism - comunismo

Notes

VocExplain: "He" in Spanish is a false cognate for the English word "he." In Spanish, it means "I have," followed by an action.

183

Take it easy. Don't work too hard.

Tómalo con calma. No trabajes tan duro.

Tómalo - take it
con - with
calma - ease
no - do not
trabajes - work
tan - so
duro - hard

Vocabulary

hard work - trabajo duro
effort - esfuerzo
burned out - cansado
labor - labor
task - quehacer
shift - turno
swamped - inundado
overtime - horas extra
anti-social - antisocial
quitting - renunciar
take a leave - tomar descanso
example - ejemplo

184

What about you?

¿Qué pasa contigo?

Qué - what
pasa - is going on
contigo - with you

Vocabulary

chitchat - charlar
mood - ánimo
mind - mente
so-so - mas o menos
not in a good mood - de mal humor
happy - alegre
lazy - perezoso
relax - relajar
tranquil - tranquilo
inactive - inactivo

Notes

Grammar: "Pasa" is the second person singular present form of "pasar," which means "to pass" or "to happen."

185

Just busy with my kids

Solamente ocupado(m)/ocupada(f) con mis hijos

Solamente - just
ocupado(m)/ocupada(f) - busy
con - with
mis hijos - my kids

Vocabulary

home life - vida hogareña
shenanigan - shenanigan
make a fool - hacer el ridículo
joke - chiste
careful - cuidadoso
careless - descuidado
smack - golpe
fall down - caer
bleeding - sangrando
bandage - vendaje

Notes

Grammar: "Hijos" is masculine because it is plural. For many words, the default gender when they are plural is the masculine gender.

186

How old are they now?

¿Cuantos años tienen ahora?

Cuantos - how many
años - years
tienen - do they have
ahora - now

Vocabulary

I don't know - no se
find out - enterar
question - pregunta
community - comunidad
lack of information - falta de información
answer - respuesta
inquire - pregunta
disobedient - desobediente
parks - parques

Notes

Grammar: "Tienen" is the third person plural present form of the verb "tener," meaning "to have"

187

My son is 5 and my daughter is 3

Mi hijo tiene cinco años y mi hija tiene tres años

Mi hijo - my son	años - years
tiene - has	y mi hija - and my daughter
cinco - five	tres - three

Vocabulary

freedom - libertad	**mashed food** - comida triturada
not in control - no en control	**young ones** - jóvenes
tolerate - tolerar	**amenable** - dócil
grow up fast - crecer rápido	**active** - activo
diet - dieta	

Notes

Culture: Kindergarten in Spanish is called "kinder" or "jardín"

188

Give them my love

Dales mi cariño

Dales - give them	mi cariño - my love/care

Vocabulary

tenderness - ternura	**similarities** - similitudes
embrace - abrazar	**very large** - muy grande
boy/girl - niño/a	**very small** - muy pequeño
differences - diferencias	**different** - diferente

Notes

Grammar: "Dales" is an imperative form of "dar," or "to give." "Dar" is an irregular verb - other forms are "doy" ("I give"), "das" ("you give"), "da" ("he/she gives"), "damos" ("we give"), "dan" ("you (pl.)/they give").

189

We should get together for a dinner

Nos deberíamos reunir para una cena

Nos - we	para - for
deberíamos - should	una - a
reunir - get together	cena - dinner

Vocabulary

friends - amistades	**lie** - mentir
promise - promesa	**either** - cualquier
agreement - acuerdo	**neither** - ningún

Notes

Culture: Group dinners among friends are common. One person will usually offer to pay for everyone, with the understanding that someone else will offer next time.

190

Sounds great

Suena genial

Suena - sounds	genial - great

Vocabulary

chant - canto	**dine** - cenar
speak - platicar	**wine** - vino
considerate - considerado	**date** - cita
excited - entusiasmado	**dish** - plato
praise - elogiar	**street food** - comida de calle
sympathetic - simpático	**oil** - aceite

Notes

VocExplain: "Me parece bien" is another common way to express the same sentiment and roughly means "it seems good to me".

191

What kind of food do you like?

¿Qué tipo de comida te gusta?

Qué - what	comida - food
tipo - kind/type	te - you
de - of	gusta - like

Vocabulary

prefer - preferir	**protein** - proteína
seafood - mariscos	**flavor** - sabor
carbs - carbohidratos	**roast** - asado
fat - grasa	**steamed** - al vapor

Notes

Culture: Cuisines in Latin America are very diverse and vary a lot from country to country and even regionally within the same country.

192

I love BBQ

Me encanta la barbacoa

Me encanta - I love	barbacoa - BBQ
la - the	

Vocabulary

beans - frijoles	**steam** - vapor
lentils - lentejas	**group** - grupo
raw - crudo	**garbage** - basura
clay pot - maceta de barro	**over cooked** - sobrecocido
slow cook - cocinar a fuego lento	**spices** - especies

Notes

Culture: In many parts of Latin America, grilled food and "carne asada" are very popular

193

How about we go for a family picnic?

¿Qué tal si vamos de picnic en familia?

Qué tal - how about
si - if
vamos - we go
de - on a
picnic - picnic
en familia - as a family

Vocabulary

camping - campamento
tent - tienda de campaña
outside - afuera
basket - canasta
torch - linterna
table cloth - mantel
fold - doblar
unfold - desplegar

Notes

Talk: "Qué tal" by itself can be used to mean "how's it going?" In this context, however, it means "how about"

194

That would be fun

Eso sería divertido

Eso - that
sería - would be
divertido - fun

Vocabulary

captivate - captivar
indulge - complacer
stimulate - estimular
tickle - hacer cosquillas
must be fun - debe ser divertido
disposable plates - platos desechables
comic - cómico
entertain - entretener
amused - entretenido
delight - deleite
gratify - satisfacer
mat - tapete

Notes

Grammar: "Sería" is from "ser," the more permanent state of being.

195

Let me talk to my wife to set a date

Déjame hablar con mi esposa para fijar una fecha

Déjame - let me	mi esposa - my wife
hablar - talk	para fijar - to set
con - with	una fecha - a date

Vocabulary

calendar - calendario	**quarter** - cuarto
century - siglo	**span** - lapso
year - año	**term** - término
month - mes	**week** - semana
period - periodo	**dates** - dátiles

Notes

Grammar: "Déjame" is an imperative verb meaning "allow me"

196

How is your brother?

¿Cómo está tu hermano?

Cómo - how	tu - your
está - is	hermano - brother

Vocabulary

phone number - número telefónico	**greet** - saludar
schoolmates - compañeros de escuela	**my regards** - mis saludos
contact - contactar	**shut off** - desconectar
give regards - dar saludos	**companion** - compañero
email address - dirección de correo electrónico	

Notes

Grammar: "Hermano" is "brother" so it is masculine, whereas "hermana" means sister so it is feminine

197

He moved to Chile for work

Se mudó a Chile por el trabajo

Se - he	por - for
mudó - moved	el - the
a - to	trabajo - work

Vocabulary

profession - profesión	**permission** - permiso
business trip - viaje de negocios	**not allowed** - no permitido
visit visa - visa de extranjero	**visa stamp** - sello de visa
foreign worker - trabajador del extranjero	**livelihood** - sustento

Notes

Grammar: "Mudó" is the third person plural past form of "mudar," which means "to move" in the context of relocating residence.

198

Is he on Facebook?

¿Él está en Facebook?

Él - he	en - on
está - is	

Vocabulary

changing times - épocas de cambio	**television** - televisión
social order - orden social	**computer** - computadora
internet - la red	**dictatorship** - dictadura
send message - mandar mensaje	**socialist** - socialista
like photo - gustar foto	**conversation** - conversación

Notes

Culture: Facebook and WhatsApp are two very popular forms of communication in Latin America

199

Yes, you can send him a friend request

Sí, puedes enviarle una solicitud de amistad

Sí - yes
puedes - you can
enviarle - send him
una solicitud - a request
de - of
amistad - friendship

Vocabulary

beg - mendigar
beggar - mendigo
implore - implorar
plead - alegar
social media - medios de comunicación social
mail - correo
receive - recibir
send - mandar
mobile phone - móvil
battery - pila

Notes

VocExplain: "Mandarle" can also be used in place of "enviarle"

200

Let's keep in touch

Quedémonos en contacto

Quedémonos - let us stay
en - in
contacto - contact

Vocabulary

global village - aldea global
humanity - humanidad
meeting - junta
united - unido
divided - dividido

Notes

Grammar: "Quedémonos" is 1st person plural present imperative form of "quedar," or "to stay." Other forms of "quedar" are "quedo" ("I stay"), "quedas" ("you stay"), "queda" ("he/she stays"), "quedamos" ("we stay"), "quedan"("you (pl.)/they stay").

Friends For Life
Amigos De Por Vida

Humans are fundamentally social creatures who learn, grow, and thrive through strong social bonds.

Los seres humanos son criaturas fundamentalmente sociales que aprenden, crecen y prosperan a través de fuertes vínculos sociales.

The fast pace of modern life can sometimes overwhelm us, and we start ignoring our social needs.

El ritmo rápido de la vida moderna a veces puede abrumarnos y comenzamos a ignorar nuestras necesidades sociales.

This can result in declining mental and physical health.

Esto puede resultar en una disminución de la salud mental y física.

Taking time to socialize with friends has a positive effect on our overall health.

Tomar tiempo para socializar con amigos tiene un efecto positivo en nuestra salud general.

The advent of social media has had a positive as well as a negative impact.

El advenimiento de las redes sociales ha tenido un impacto tanto positivo como negativo.

On the one hand, it has enabled people to stay connected across vast distances, but on the other hand, it has reduced in-person socialization.

Por un lado, ha permitido a las personas mantenerse conectadas a través de grandes distancias, pero por otro lado, ha reducido la socialización en persona.

By taking the time to meet with people and talking about family, career, and interests, you feel happy.

Al tomar tiempo para reunirse con gente y hablar sobre la familia, la carrera y los intereses, uno se siente feliz.

When life throws you a challenge, it is easier to face it if you are surrounded by friends and family.

Cuando la vida te lanza un desafío, es más fácil enfrentarlo si estás rodeado de amigos y familiares.

We should all be thankful for the true friends in our life.

Todos debemos estar agradecidos por los verdaderos amigos en nuestra vida.

Read and Recall Meaning

181. Hola amigo(m)/amiga(f). ¿En dónde has estado?

amistad
mejores amigos
amigo de la niñez
duradero
corta vida
reunión
enemigo
adversario

182. He estado ocupado(m)/ocupada(f) con el trabajo

ocupado
presión
estrés
analista político
elecciones
opinión popular
socialismo
comunismo

183. Tómalo con calma. No trabajes tan duro.

trabajo duro
esfuerzo
cansado
labor
quehacer
turno
inundado
horas extra
antisocial
renunciar
tomar descanso
ejemplo

184. ¿Qué pasa contigo?

charlar
ánimo
mente
mas o menos
de mal humor
alegre
perezoso
relajar
tranquilo
inactivo

185. Solamente ocupado(m)/ocupada(f) con mis hijos

vida hogareña
shenanigan
hacer el ridículo
chiste
cuidadoso
descuidado
golpe
caer

sangrando
vendaje

186. ¿Cuantos años tienen ahora?

no se
enterar
pregunta
comunidad
falta de información
respuesta
pregunta
desobediente
parques

187. Mi hijo tiene cinco años y mi hija tiene tres años

libertad
no en control
tolerar
crecer rápido
dieta
comida triturada
jóvenes
dócil
activo

188. Dales mi cariño

ternura
abrazar
niño/a
diferencias
similitudes
muy grande
muy pequeño
diferente

189. Nos deberíamos reunir para una cena

amistades
promesa
acuerdo
mentir
cualquier
ningún

190. Suena genial

canto
platicar
considerado
entusiasmado
elogiar
simpático
cenar
vino
cita
plato
comida de calle
aceite

191. ¿Qué tipo de comida te gusta?

preferir
mariscos
carbohidratos
grasa

proteína
sabor
asado
al vapor

192. Me encanta la barbacoa

frijoles
lentejas
crudo
maceta de barro
cocinar a fuego lento
vapor
grupo
basura
sobrecocido
especies

193. ¿Qué tal si vamos de picnic en familia?

campamento
tienda de campaña
afuera
canasta
linterna
mantel
doblar
desplegar

194. Eso sería divertido

captivar
complacer
estimular
hacer cosquillas
debe ser divertido
platos desechables
cómico
entretener
entretenido
deleite
satisfacer
tapete

195. Déjame hablar con mi esposa para fijar una fecha

calendario
siglo
año
mes
periodo
cuarto
lapso
término
semana
dátiles

196. ¿Cómo está tu hermano?

número telefónico
compañeros de escuela
contactar
dar saludos
dirección de correo
electrónico
saludar
mis saludos
desconectar
compañero

197. Se mudó a Chile por el trabajo

profesión	permiso
viaje de negocios	no permitido
visa de extranjero	sello de visa
trabajador del extranjero	sustento

198. ¿El está en Facebook?

épocas de cambio	televisión
orden social	computadora
la red	dictadura
mandar mensaje	socialista
gustar foto	conversación

199. Sí, puedes enviarle una solicitud de amistad

mendigar	correo
mendigo	recibir
implorar	mandar
alegar	móvil
medios de comunicación social	pila

200. Quedémonos en contacto

aldea global	unido
humanidad	dividido
junta	

Grammar Tables

"Get the fundamentals down and the level of everything you do will rise."

"Domina los fundamentos y el nivel de todo lo que hagas se elevará."

Michael Jordan
American basketball player
(b 1963)

Questions

what	qué
when	cuándo
why	porqué
where	dónde
which	cuál
who	quien
whom	quien
whose	de quien
how	cómo
how much	cuanto
how many	cuantos
is it	es
are you	eres

Saying no

yes	sí
no	no
not	no
none	ningún
never	nunca

Joining Words

and	y
but	pero
or	o
if	si
whether	ya sea
on	en
from	de
for	para/por

Count

first	primer/o/a
second	segundo/a
third	tercer/o/a
fourth	cuarto/a
fifth	quinto/a
less	menos
more	más

Pronouns

I	yo
we	nosotros
you	tú
he	él
she	ella
they	ellos
it	él

Demonstratives

this	esto
that	eso
these	estos
those	esos

Possessives

my	mi
our	nuestro
your	tu
his	de él
her	de ella
their	de ellos
it's	su

More Possessives

mine	mio
ours	nuestro
yours	tuyo
his	suyo
hers	suyo
theirs	suyo

Object

me	yo
us	nosotros
you	tú
him	él
her	ella
them	ellos

Present Tense

to be (simple)

I am	soy
we are	somos
you are	eres
he is	es
she is	es
they are	son

to do (simple)

I do	hago
we do	hacemos
you do	haces
he does	hace
she does	hace
they do	hacen

to do (continuous)

I am doing	estoy haciendo
we are doing	estamos haciendo
you are doing	estás haciendo
he is doing	está haciendo
she is doing	está haciendo
they are doing	estan haciendo

to do (perfect)

I have done	he hecho
we have done	hemos hecho
you have done	has hecho
he has done	ha hecho
she has done	ha hecho
they have done	han hecho

to eat (simple)

I eat	como
we eat	comemos
you eat	comes
he eats	come
she eats	come
they eat	comen

to eat (continuous)

I am eating	estoy comiendo
we are eating	estamos comiendo
you are eating	estás comiendo
he is eating	está comiendo
she is eating	está comiendo
they are eating	están comiendo

to eat (perfect)

I have eaten	he comido
we have eaten	hemos comido
you have eaten	has comido
he has eaten	ha comido
she has eaten	ha comido

they have eaten han comido

Past Tense

to be (simple)

I was fuí
we were fuimos
you were fuiste
he was fue
she was fue
they were fueron

to do (simple)

I did hice
we did hicimos
you did hiciste
he did hizo
she did hizo
they did hicieron

to do (continuous)

I was doing estaba haciendo
we were doing estábamos haciendo
you were doing estabas haciendo
he was doing estaba haciendo
she was doing estaba haciendo
they were doing estaban haciendo

to do (perfect)

I had done había hecho
we had done habíamos hecho
you had done habías hecho
he had done había hecho
she had done había hecho
they had done habían hecho

to eat (simple)

I ate comí
we ate comimos
you ate comiste
he ate comió
she ate comió
they ate comieron

to eat (continuous)

I was eating estaba comiendo
we were eating estábamos comiendo
you were eating estabas comiendo
he was eating estaba comiendo
she was eating estaba comiendo
they were eating estaban comiendo

to eat (perfect)

I had eaten había comido
we had eaten habíamos comido

you had eaten	habías comido
he had eaten	había comido
she had eaten	había comido
they had eaten	habían comido

Future Tense

to be

I will	iré
we will	iremos
you will	irás
he will	irá
she will	irá
they will	irán

to do

I will do	iré hacer
we will do	iremos hacer
you will do	irás hacer
he will do	irá hacer
she will do	irá hacer
they will do	irán hacer

to eat

I will eat	comeré
we will eat	comeremos
you will eat	comerás
he will eat	comerá
she will eat	comerá
they will eat	comerán

English to Spanish Dictionary

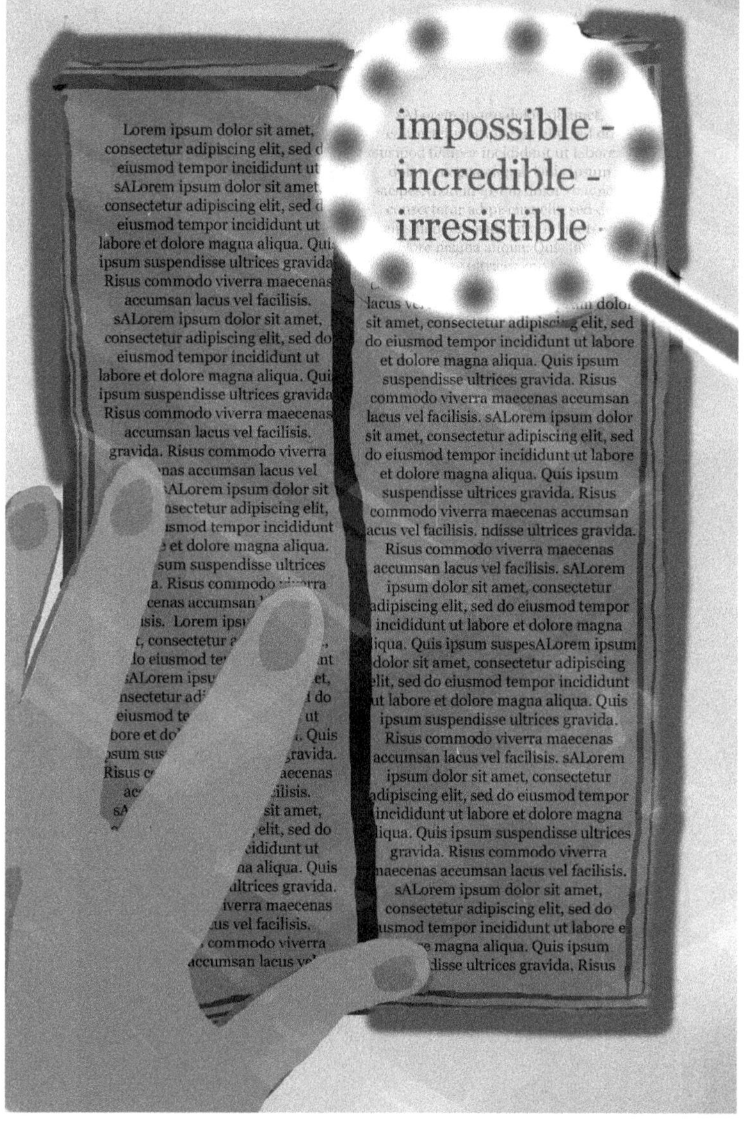

"Impossible is a word to be found only in the dictionary of fools."

"Imposible es una palabra que se encuentra solo en el diccionario de los tontos."

Napoleon Bonaparte
French military leader
(1769 – 1821)

A

12 o clock - las doce del día
a - un/una
above - encima
above the clouds - sobre las nubes
abroad - en el extranjero
abusive - abusivo/a
to accelerate - acelerar
acceptance - aceptación
accident - accidente
action movie - película de acción
active - activo
activities - ocupaciones
actor - actor
acupuncture - acupuntura
acute - agudo
to add - sumar
address - dirección
to admire - admirar
admission - admisión
admission criteria - criterios de admisión
admission officer - oficial de admisión
to adore - adorar
adult - adulto
advantage - ventaja
adventure - aventura
affection - afecto
affinity - afinidad
affordable - barato/asequible
afraid - asustado
after - después
afternoon - tardes
again - de nuevo
age - edad
age gap - diferencia de edad
ages - siglos
aggressive - agresivo
agnostic - agnóstico
August - agosto
I agree - estoy de acuerdo
agreement - acuerdo
air - aire
air pressure - presión del aire
airplane - avión
airport - aeropuerto
aisle seat - asiento de pasillo
alarm - alarma
allow me - dame permiso
allowed - permitido
not allowed - no permitido
almonds - almendras
alone - solitario/a
also - También
always - siempre
amazing - asombroso/increíble
ambulance - ambulancia
amenable - amable/dócil
north America - Norteamérica
American - americano
tonsils - amígdalas
amused - entretenido
ancestors - antepasados
and - y
anger - enojo
animal - animal
ankles - tobillos
anniversary - aniversario
to annoy - fastidiar

to answer - respuesta
Anteayer - Day before Yesterday
anthem - himno
anti-social - antisocial
to anticipate - prever
antique - antiguo
apology - disculpa
appearance - apariencia
appetizer - entrada
apple - manzana
application deadline - plazo de solicitud
to appreciate - apreciar
April - abril
architecture - arquitectura
area - área
Argentinian - argentino
argument - pleito
arrival - llegada
arrogant - arrogante
art - arte
arthritis - artritis
as a family - en familia
as well - también
Asian - asiático
Asian influence - influencia asiática
to ask for - pedir
assistant professor - profesor asistente
atlantic ocean - océano atlántico
attachment - fijación
you attend - asistes
I attend - Asisto
attention-seeking - buscando atención
attractions - atracciones
attractive - atractivo
auction - subasta
aunt - tía
authentic - auténtico
author - autor
availability - disponibilidad
available - disponible
not available - no disponible
to avoid - evitar
awesome - chido/a / impresionante

B

baby - bebé
back seats - asientos traseros
backpack - mochila
bad - mal
bag - bolsa
bag - maleta
baked goods - productos horneados
bakery - panadería
baking - hornear
balance - equilibrio
balance - saldo
balanced diet - dieta equilibrada
balcony - balcón
bald - calvo
ball - pelota
balloons - globos
ballpoint - bolígrafo
banana - plátano
bandage - vendaje
bank - banco
barber shop - barbería
barely know them - apenas

le conozco
bargain (n) - ganga
to bark - ladrar
basket - canasta
basketball - baloncesto
battery - pila
BBQ - barbacoa
beach - playa
bean soup - sopa de frijol
beans - frijoles
beard - barba
beautiful - hermoso/a
beauty - belleza
becoming night - anochecer
bed - cama
bedroom - habitación
bedsheet - sábana
beef - carne de res
beef noodle - fideos de res
before - antes
to beg - mendigar
beggar - mendigo
behind - detrás
beliefs - creencias
below - abajo/bajo
belt - cinturón
beneath - debajo
benevolent - benévolo/a
besides - además
best - superior
best man - padrino de boda
best-seller - el éxito de librería
besties - mejores amigos
better - mejor
beverage - bebida
bicycle - bicicleta
big - grande
biography - biografía
birds - aves
birthday - cumpleaños
birthplace - lugar de nacimiento
bite - mordida
black - negro
bland - poco fuerte
bleeding - sangrando
blessed - bendito/a
blind - siego/a
blood - sangre
blue - azul (s)
blue - azules (p)
boarding gate - puerta de abordaje
boca - mouth
boil - hervir
boiling water - agua hervida
bone - hueso
bonus - extra
book - libro
booking - reserva
booklet - libreta
bookstore - librería
boots - botas
boring - aburrido
born - nacer
to borrow - pedir prestado
boss - jefe
to bother - molestar
bottle - botella
bowl - bol
boy/girl - niño/a
bra - sostén
brain - cerebro
brake - freno
brave - valiente

bread - pan
breakfast - desayuno
breast piece - pechuga
breastfeeding - amamantamiento
to breathe - respirar
bride - novia
bridesmaid - dama de honor
briefcase - maletín
bright - brillante
to bring - traer
British - británico
British pound - libra británica
broccoli - brócoli
brother - hermano
brother-in-law - cuñado
brotherhood - fraternidad
brown - café
Buddhism - budismo
budget - presupuesto
buildings - edificios
bump into - encontrarse con
bumpy ride - paseo lleno de baches
bureaucrat - burócrata
burn - quemar
burned out - cansado
burp - eructar
bus - autobús
bus station - estación de autobús
business - negocios
business center - centro de negocios
business trip - viaje de negocios
businessman - empresario
busy - ocupado/a
busy season - temporada ocupada
butter - mantequilla
button - botón
to buy - comprar
by sea - en barco

C

cab driver - taxista
cab fare - tarifa de taxi
cake - pastel
calculate - calcular
calendar - calendario
call him - llamarlo
calm - sereno/tranquilo
calves - pantorrillas
camera - cámara
camping - campamento
campus - campus
can I - Puedo
can you - Puedes
cancel it - cancélalo
candy shop - tienda de dulces
cap - gorra
capital - capital
captivate - captivar
car - carro
car registration - registración de auto
carbs - carbohidratos
cards - tarjetas
careful - cuidadoso
careless - descuidado
caress - acariciar
caring - cariñoso
carry - cargar

carry-on - bolso de mano
cartoon - caricatura
carts - carritos
cashier - cajero
cat - gato
catch up on sleep - alcanzar el sueño
Catholic - Católico
celebrate - celebrar
celebration - celebración
cents - centavos
century - siglo
cepillo de dientes - toothbrush
the chair - la silla
challenges - retos
chance encounter - encuentro casual
to change - cambiar
change - cambio
change of plans - cambio de planes
changing times - épocas de cambio
chant - canto
charged - cargado
charitable - caritativo
charming - encantador/a
cheap - barato (s)
cheap - baratos (p)
cheating - trampa
check - cheque
check/bill - cuenta
checkout - salida
cheeks - cachetes
cheese - queso
chew - masticar
chicken - pollo
chicken soup - sopa de pollo
child - niño
child safety seat - asiento de seguridad para niños
childhood - niñez
childhood friend - amigo de la niñez
childish - infantil
my children - Mis hijos
chitchat - charlar
chops - chuletas
Christian - cristiano
Christmas - Navidad
chronic - crónico
church - iglesia
citizen - ciudadano
city - ciudad
city center - centro
city center - centro de ciudad
city tour - paseo por la ciudad
class size - tamaño de la clase
classical - clásica
clay pot - maceta de barro
cleanliness - limpieza
climate - clima
climbing - trepando
clinic - clínica
clock - reloj
not close - no cerca
close it - ciérralo
clothing - ropa
clothing size - talla de ropa
cloud - nube
cloudy - nublado
clown - payaso

coal - carbón
coat - abrigo
coffee - café
coins - monedas
cold - frío
collar - collar/cuello
collect my things - recoger mis cosas
collected - coleccionado
color - color
colorful - colorido
colorful personality - personalidad colorida
I comb - Peino
comedy - comedia
comfortable - cómodo
comic - cómico
common ailments - dolencias comunes
common humanity - humanidad común
commotion - conmoción
communism - comunismo
community - comunidad
commute - conmutar
companion - compañero
compare - comparar
compassion - compasión
compete - rivalizar
competition - competencia
complain - quejar
complementary - complementario
computer - computadora
condition - condición
conference room - sala de conferencia
confident - confidente
congratulations - felicidades
connecting flight - vuelo de conexión
conscious - consciente
consequence - consecuencia
conservative - conservador
considerate - considerado
contact (n) - contacto
contact (v) - contactar
contract - contrato
not in control - no en control
conversation - conversación
slow cooked - cocinado a fuego lento
slow cook - cocinar a fuego lento
I cook - Cocino
cooking - cocinar
correct - correcta
it costs - Cuesta
cotton - algodón
couch - sofá
cough - tos
country - país
courage - coraje
cousin - primo/a
coward - cobarde
crafts - artesanías
create a mess - crear un lío
credit card - tarjeta de crédito
crows - cuervos
cry - llorar
Cuarto - fourth
Cuatro veces - four times
cucumber - pepino
cuddle - abrazar/acariciar

cultural differences - diferencias culturales
cultural experiences - experiencias culturales
cultural festivals - ferias culturales
cup - taza
cupboard - alacena
curly hair - cabello rizado
currency - moneda
cursed - maldito/a
cushion - colchón/colchoneta
customer service - servicio al cliente
customs - costumbres
cut - cortar
cute - lindo/a

D

daily routine - rutina cotidiana
dance - bailar
danger - peligro
dark - oscuro
dark-skinned - morena
date - cita
date - fecha
dates - dátiles
daughter - hija
daughter-in-law - nuera
dawn - madrugada
day - día (s)
day - días (p)
day off - día de descanso
dean - decano
death anniversary - aniversario de muerte
debit card - tarjeta de débito
December - diciembre
decent - decente
deduct - deducir
deep sleep - sueño profundo
deeply engrossed - profundamente absorto
delicate things - cosas delicadas
delicious - deliciosa
delight - deleite
demand - demanda
dementia - demencia
democracy - democracia
denim jacket - chaqueta de mezclilla
dentist - dentista
department stores - tiendas de departamentos
departments - departamentos
departure - partida
deposit - deposito
depressed - deprimido/a
desert - desierto
design - diseño
dessert - postre
destination - destino
diabetes - diabetes
diaper change - cambio de pañal
diarrhea - diarrea
dictatorship - dictadura
died - murió
diet - dieta
differences - diferencias
different - diferente
different cuisine - cocina

diferente
difficult - difícil
dine - cenar
dinner - cena
dinner table - mesa del comedor
direct - directo
directions - direcciones
director - director
disabled - discapacitado
disadvantage - desventaja
I disagree - no estoy de acuerdo
disaster - desastre
discount - descuento
discover - descubrir
discuss - discutir
dish - plato
dishwasher - lavador de platos
dislike - disgusto
dislikes - aversiones
disobedient - desobediente
disposable plates - platos desechables
disrespect - falta de respeto
distant relatives - parientes lejanos
divide - dividir
divided - dividido
divorced - divorciado/a
do nothing - hacer nada
Doble - double
doctor - doctor
doctor - médico
does it cost - cuesta
dog - perro
dollars - dólares
donations - donaciones
door - puerta
dos veces - twice
double bed - cama doble
double layered - doble capa
down - abajo
downpour - aguacero
dowry - dote
doze off - dormitar
drain - drenar
drawing - dibujar
dream - soñar
dress - vestido
drink (n) - beber
I drink - Tomo
I drive - Manejo
drizzle - llovizna
drop-off service - servicio de entrega
drowsy - soñoliento/a
drum sticks - patas de pollo
dry - seca
duckling - anadón
dumb - tonto/a
dumplings - empanadillas
duration - duración
dusk - la anochecida
duties - deberes
duty free - libre de impuestos

E

eagle - águila
early - temprano
early schooling - educación temprana
earrings - aretes
earth - tierra

earthquake - terremoto
ease - calma
east Asia - Asia del este
easy - fácil
easy-going - buena onda
to eat - comer
I eat - Como
eatery - restaurante
eating disorder - desorden alimenticio
eating out - comer afuera
economical - económico
economics - ciencias económicas
education - educación
effort - esfuerzo
eggs - huevos
either - cualquier
elbow - codo
elderly - anciano
elections - elecciones
electronics - electrónicos
elegance - elegancia
elementary school - escuela primaria
elevator - elevador
email address - dirección de correo electrónico
embrace - abrazar
emergency - emergencia
emotional - emocional
employ - emplear
employed - empleado
employer - empleador
employment - empleo
empty pockets - bolsillos vacíos
emulate - emular
encías - gums
end - fin
ends - fines
enemy - enemigo
energy - energía
to get engaged - de comprometer
engagement - compromiso
engaging - atractivo/cautivador/a
engineer - ingeniero/a
engineering - ingeniería
enjoy - disfrutar
enjoyment - gozo
enormous - enorme
enroll - inscribir
entertain - entretener
entrance - entrada/ingreso
entrance fee - precio de la entrada
entrepreneur - emprendedor
envelop - sobre
epidemic - epidemia
equal - igual
equally - Igualmente
español - spanish
essay - ensayo
ethnicity - etnicidad
Europe - Europa
European - europeo
European touch - toque europeo
evening - tarde
evening/night - noche
eventful - memorable
example - ejemplo
excellent - excelente
exchange rate - tipo de

cambio
excited - entusiasmado
exercise - ejercicio
exhausted - exhausto
to exit - salir
exotic food - comida exótica
expand - expandir
expectation - expectativa
expenses - gastos
expensive - caro
expertise - pericia
export - exportar
expressive - expresivo/a
extended family - familia extendida
extra charge - carga extra
extrovert - extrovertido/a
eyes - ojos
eyesight problems - problemas de la vista

F

factory price - precio de fábrica
fail - fallar
faint - desmayar
fair-skinned - piel blanca
fake - falso
fall - otoño
fall down - caer
familiarity - familiaridad
family - familia
family members - miembros de la familia
family planning - planificación familiar
family portrait - retrato familiar
family tree - árbol de familia
famous - famoso
far east - lejano este
fare - tarifa
farewell - despedida
farmer's market - mercado de agricultores
fart - pedo
fast - rápido/a
fasting - ayuno
fat - gordo
fat - grasa
father - padre
father-in-law - suegro
favorite - favorito
February - febrero
fee - cuota
feed - dar de comer
to feel - sentir
I feel - siento
feelings - sentimientos
feet - pies
female - hembra
feminine - femenina/o
festive mood - actitud festiva
fever - fiebre
fiancé/boyfriend - novio
fifty - cincuenta
fifty eight - cincuenta y ocho
fight - pelear
fill the form - llenar la forma
fill the tank - llenar el tanque
final exams - exámenes finales
find out - enterar
fine - bien

fingers - dedos
fire station - estación de bomberos
fireworks - fuegos artificiales
first name - primer nombre
first time - primera vez
first-aid station - estación de primeros auxilios
first-time - primera vez
fish soup - sopa de pescado
fitness - estado físico
fitting - ajustado
five - cinco
five hundred - quinientos
flag - bandera
flavor - sabor
flight - vuelo
flight attendant - aeromozo
flight status - estado del vuelo
flight time - tiempo de vuelo
flip flop - chancla
flood - Inundación
floss - hilo dental
flowers - las flores
flush the toilet - echar agua al excusado
fly - volar
flying - volando
fold - doblar
folding chair - silla plegable
folk music - música folklórica
food - comida
football - fútbol
foreign - extranjeras
foreign worker - trabajador del extranjero
foreigner - extranjero/a
forest - bosque
forget - olvidar
forgive me - perdóname
forgive/excuse me - Disculpe
forgot - olvidé
fork - tenedor
formal - formal
formal/permanent - Adios
formality - formalidad
fortunate - afortunado
forty seven - cuarenta y siete
fountain pen - pluma fuente
fraction - fracción
frail - débil
free time - tiempo libre
freedom - libertad
frequently - frecuentemente
fresh - fresco
Friday - viernes
fried - freído
friend - amigo(m)/amiga(f)
friendly - amistoso/simpático
friends - amistades
friendship - amistad
new friendships - nuevas amistades
fries - papas fritas
from - De
front seats - asientos delanteros
frozen - congelado
fruit - fruta
frustrated - frustrado
fry - freír

fuel indicator - indicador de combustible
fuel station - gasolinera
to be full - estar satisfecho
full - satisfecho/a
fun - divertido
function - función
funds - fondos
funeral - velorio
funny - gracioso/a
fur - piel/pelaje

G

game - juego
garbage - basura
garlic - ajo
gathering - Reunir
gender - género
new generation - nueva generación
generous - generoso
gentleman - caballero
genuine - genuino
get off from work - salir del trabajo
get together - reunir
getting dark - oscurecer
getting late - volviendo tarde
gift - regalo
gift shop - tienda de regalos
gifts - regalos
ginger - jengibre
girlfriends - amigas
give - dar
give regards - dar saludos
give them - Dales
glass - vaso
glasses - gafas
global village - aldea global
gloves - guantes
to go - ir
we go - vamos
go - Ve
I go - Voy
go fast - ir rápido
go out - salir
goals - metas
god - dios
golden - dorado
good - buen (s)(neuter)
good - buena (f)
good - buenas (p)(f)
good - bueno
good - buenos (p)(m)
not good - no bueno
good character - buen carácter
good deal - buena oferta
good times - buenos tiempos
goose - ganso
government office - oficina gubernamental
government official - funcionario del gobierno
graceful - agraciado/a
graduation - graduación
granddaughter - nieta
grandfather - abuelo
grandmother - abuela
grandson - nieto
grass - pasto
to be grateful - estar agradecido/a
gratify - satisfacer
great - genial

great service - servicio genial
greedy - codicioso
green - verde
greet - saludar
greetings - saludos
grey hair - cabello gris
grill - parrilla
groceries - comestibles
groom - novio
ground floor - planta baja
group - grupo
grow up - crecer
grow up fast - crecer rápido
guests - invitados
gums - encías

H

habits - hábitos
haggle - regatear
hail - granizo
hair - cabello
haircut - corte de pelo
hairdresser - peluquero
hairstyle - peinado
hairy - peludo
half - media
half-brother - medio hermano
half-hour - media hora
half-price - medio precio
hand soap - jabón para manos
hands - manos
handsome - guapo
hangout - pasar el rato
happy - alegre
happy - feliz
hard - duro
hard life - vida difícil
hard-of-hearing - duro de oído
hard-work - trabajo duro
hard-working - trabajador/a
has - tiene
hat - sombrero
hatch - eclosionar
I hate - odio
hatred - odio
to have - tener
I have - Tengo
you have - tienes
have to - tener que
he - el
headache - dolor de cabeza
headband - diadema
headscarf - barbijo
health - salud
healthy - saludable
healthy eating - alimentación saludable
hear - escuchar
heart - corazón
heart attack - ataque al corazón
heart patient - paciente del corazón
heart-broken - corazón roto
heartbeat - latido del corazón
heat - calor
heavy meal - comida pesada
height - altura
hell - infierno
hello - Hola
helmet - casco

help - ayuda
her - ella
here - aquí
high heel - tacón alto
high position - posición alta
high school - escuela preparatoria
high standard - alto nivel
highway fee - tarifa de carretera
hiking - excursiones
hilo dental - floss
his - Su
historic sites - sitios históricos
hold it - tenerlo
hole - hueco
holiday - feriado
holy book - libro sagrado
home - hogar
home cooked - cocinado en casa
home life - vida hogareña
homework - tarea
honesty - honestidad
hoodie - capucha
I hope - Espero
my hopes - mis esperanzas
horizon - horizonte
horrible - horrible
horror film - película de terror
horse - caballo
hospital - hospital
hostels - hostales
hot - caliente
hot - caluroso
hotel - hotel
house - casa
how - Cómo
how far? - qué lejos
how long? - cuanto tiempo
how many - Cuantos
how much - Cuanto
how's it going? - ¿Qué tal?
Hoy - today
hug - abrazo
human connection - conexión humana
human resources - recursos humanos
humanities - humanidades
humanity - humanidad
humble - humilde
humidity - humedad
humor - humor
hundred - ciento
hunger - hambre
in a hurry - apurado
hurry up - apúrate
hurry up - darse prisa
hurt - lastimado
husband - marido

I

I - Yo
I am - Estoy
I am - Soy
ice - hielo
ice cream - helado
id card - tarjeta de identificación
if - si
ignorant - ignorante
ignore - ignorar
ill - enfermo/mal

illegal - ilegal
illness - enfermedad
imagination - imaginación
immature - inmaduro/a
immediately - inmediatamente
implore - implorar
impolite - descortés
import - importar
impressive - impresionante
in - en
in-law - suegros
inactive - inactivo
incentives - incentivos
inches - pulgadas
inclination - inclinación
independent - independiente
Indian - indio
indian ocean - océano indio
indulge - complacer
infant - infante
informal - informal
informal/temporary - Chao
information - información
information center - centro de información
infrequent visits - visitas infrecuentes
inheritance - herencia
inhumane - inhumano/a
injured - lesionado/lastimado
ink - tinta
inquire - pregunta
instantly - instantemente
insurance - seguro
integrity - integridad
intelligent - inteligente
interest rate - tasa de interés
interesting - interesante
interests - intereses
internet - la red
internet fee - tarifa de internet
introduction - introducción
introvert - introvertido
investor - inversionista
invitation - invitación
invite - invitar
invoice - factura
iron - plancha
irritate - irritar
is going on - pasa
is it - Es
is named - se llama
is there - Hay

J

jacket - chamarra
January - enero
Japanese - japonés
jaws - mandíbulas
jeans - pantalones jeans
jelly - gelatina
jewelry - joyería
Jewish faith - fe judía
job - trabajo
jogging - trotar
joke - chiste
joy - alegría
joyful - alegría/alegre
juice - jugo
July - julio
jump - brincar
jumpy - asustadizo
June - junio

just - solamente
just finished - acaba

K
kettle - tetera
key - llave
kidney - riñón
my kids - mis hijos
kin - pariente
kind - amable
kind/type - tipo
kindergarten - el kínder
kiss - beso
kitchen - cocina
knees - rodillas
knife - cuchillo
knitted hat - sombrero tejido
I don't know - no se
knowledgeable - enterado
Korean - coreano

L
labor - labor
laces - cordones
lack of energy - falta de energía
lack of information - falta de información
lake - lago
lamb - cordero
landscape - paisaje
language barrier - obstáculo lingüístico
lap - piernas
large - grande
last - pasado
last - último
last minute sale - venta de última hora
last name - apellido
late - tarde
late fee - cargo por demora
later - luego
to laugh - reír
laughter - risa
laundry - lavandería
lazy - perezoso
learn - aprender
lease - arrendamiento
leash - correa
leather - cuero
leather shoes - zapatos de cuero
to leave - irme
left - izquierda
leftovers - sobras
leg piece - pierna
leg room - espacio para las pierna
legal - legal
lend - prestar
lentils - lentejas
less - menos
let me - Déjame
let us stay - Quedémonos
liberal - liberal
library - biblioteca
lie - mentir
light - luz
light meal - comida ligera
to like - gustar
I like it - me gusta
I would like - Me gustaría
I like you - me gustas
like a brother - como un

hermano
like photo - gustar foto
likes - gustos
limp - cojear
lips - labios
liquids - líquidos
I listen to - Escucho
literature - literatura
little ones - pequeños
live - vivir
I live - Vivo
livelihood - sustento
liver - hígado
lives - vive
loan - préstamo
location - locación
lock - cerradura
lonely - solitario
long distance - a larga distancia
long hair - cabello largo
long life - larga vida
long line - fila larga
long-lasting - duradero
look alike - parecidos
to look - ver
loose - flojo
I lost - Perdí
lost and found - objetos perdidos
loud - ruidoso
lounge - salón
to love - amar
I love - amo
love - amor
I love - Me encanta
love/care - cariño
lovely - encantador
loving - cariñoso/a
low sound - ruido bajo
loyal - fiel
loyalty - lealtad
luck - suerte
lucky - suertudo
luggage - maletas
lukewarm water - agua tibia
lunch - almuerzo
lunch break - descanso para almorzar
lung cancer - cáncer de pulmón
lungs - pulmones
luxury - lujo
luxury bag - cartera de lujo

M

magazine - revista
mail - correo
main course - plato fuerte
made in France - hecho en Francia
make a fool - hacer el ridículo
make fun of - burlarse de
make use of - hacer uso de
make your bed - tender la cama
makeup - maquillaje
male - macho
malnourished - desnutrido/a
man - hombre
management fee - comisión de gestión
manly - varonil
manners - modales

many - muchos
March - marzo
marital life - vida marital
market - mercado
market fluctuate - fluctuación del mercado
marriage ceremony - ceremonia de matrimonio
married - casado/a
to get married - de casar
mashed food - comida triturada
massage - masaje
master's degree - maestría
mat - tapete
material - material
mattress - colchón
mature - maduro/a
May - mayo
maybe - quizás
me - Yo
me too - yo también
meaning - significado
measurements - mediciones
meat - carne
medical checkup - revisión médica
medical school - escuela de medicina
medicine - medicina
meet - conocer
meeting - junta
melt - derretir
memories - memorias
memory - memoria
mental - mental
mentor - mentor
menu - menú
Mexican currency - pesos
midnight - media noche
middle age - mediana edad
middle east - el medio oriente
middle school - escuela secundaria
military - ejército
milk - leche
mind - mente
mindful - consciente
Mine - mio
minute - minuto
mirror - espejo
I miss - extraño
mistake - error
mobile phone - móvil
modern - moderno
Monday - lunes
monetary policy - política monetaria
money - dinero
month - mes
monthly allowance - pensión mensual
monuments - monumentos
mood - ánimo/humor
not in a good mood - de mal humor
moon - luna
more - más
the morning - la mañana
mosque - mezquita
mother - madre
mother-in-law - suegra
motherhood - maternidad
motherly instinct - instinto materno

motorbike - moto
mountains - montañas
moustache - bigote
mouth - boca
moved - mudó
movie - película
movie theater - cine
Mr - señor
Mrs - señora
Ms - señorita
much - Mucho
mud - lodo
multiply - multiplicar
muscular - musculoso
museums - museos
music - música
music player - reproductor de música
Muslim - musulmán
must be fun - debe ser divertido
mutual respect - respeto mutuo
my (s) - Mi
my (p) - Mis

N

nails - uñas
name - nombre
nap - siesta
narrow-minded - limitado/a
nation - nación
national - nacional
nationality - nacionalidad
natural diet - dieta natural
natural food - comida natural
natural medicine - medicina natural
nature - naturaleza
naughty - travieso/a
navigate - navegar
near - cerca
near future - futuro cercano
necklace - collar
need (n) - necesidad
need to - necesitar
I need - Necesito
needle - aguja
negotiate - negociar
neighbourhood - barrio
neither - ningún
nephew - sobrino
never - nunca
never before - nunca antes
new - nuevos
new year - año nuevo
newborn - recién nacido
newly wed - recién casados
newspaper - periódico
next - próxima
next - siguiente
nick name - apodo
niece - sobrina
night - noche
night market - mercado nocturno
nightmares - pesadillas
nine - nueve
no - no
no problem - no hay problema
no thanks to you - no gracias a ti
no way - de ninguna manera
no worries - no te

preocupes
noise - ruido
non-fiction - no ficción
non-profit - el no comercial
None - ningún
noon - medio día
not - No
notebook - cuaderno
nothing - nada
novel - novela
November - noviembre
now - ahora
not now - no ahora
number one - número uno
number plate - numero de placas
nurse - enfermera
nutrients - nutrientes
nutrition - nutrición
nuts - nueces

O

oath - juramento
obedience - obediencia
obedient - obediente
to obtain - conseguir
occasionally - de vez en cuando
occupation - ocupación
ocean - océano
October - octubre
of - de
of the - del
offer - oferta
office - oficina
offices - oficinas
official taxi - taxi oficial
oil - aceite
old - viejo
old town - pueblo viejo
older - mayor
omelet - omelet
on - en
on time - a tiempo
once again - de nuevo
once again - otra vez
once before - una vez antes
one (m) - un
one (f) - una
one month old - un mes de edad
onion - cebolla
open and honest - abierto y honesto
open it - ábrelo
open-minded - libre de prejuicios
operation - operación
opponent - adversario
opportunist - oportunista
opposite - opuesto
or - o
orange - anaranjada
orange juice - jugo de naranja
order - pedir
ordinary - ordinario/a
organs - órganos
original - original
other - otro/a
our - nuestro
out of breath - sin aliento
out of country - fuera del país
out of sight - fuera de vista
outdoors - al aire libre

outside - afuera
outside the gate - fuera de la puerta
over charge - sobre carga
over cooked - sobre cocido
overweight - sobrepeso
over-stay - permanecer demasiado tiempo
overcoat - sobre todo
overlook - pasar por alto
overnight flight - vuelo nocturno
overtake - sobrepasar
overtime - horas extra
overweight - sobrepeso
own - poseer

P

pacific ocean - océano pacifico
pack - empacar
paid out - pagado
in pain - adolorido
pair - par
pajamas - pijamas
pants - pantalones
paper - papel
paper bag - bolsa de papel
paperwork - papeleo
paradise - paraíso
parents - padres
park - parque
parking - estacionamiento
parks - parques
parrot - loro
part-time - medio tiempo
party - fiesta
pass - pasar
pass me - pasarme
passengers - pasajeros
passport - pasaporte
past - pasado
pasta de dientes - toothpaste
pastimes - pasatiempos
pastures - pastos
pat down - palmadita
paws - patas
pay - pagar
I pay - Pago
pay cash - pagar con efectivo
pay in credit card - pagar con tarjeta
payment - pago
peace - paz
peanuts - cacahuates
pen - pluma
penalty - penalización
pencil - lápiz
pending errands - el quehacer pendiente
people - gente
pepper - pimienta
percent - por ciento
period - periodo
permission - permiso
personal - personal
personality - personalidad
pet - mascota
petite - chiquita
PhD - doctorado
phone - teléfono
phone call - llamada telefónica
Phone number - número telefónico

photo - foto
physical - físico/material
physique - físico
picnic - picnic
pigeon - paloma
pillow - almohada
pineapple - piña
pink - rosado
places - lugares
planning - planear
plans - planes
plants - plantas
plastic bag - bolsa de plástico
plate - plato
I play - Juego
to play - jugar
play the ball - jugar pelota
playful - juguetón
playground - patio de recreo
plead - alegar
pleasant - agradable
please - por favor
pleasure - gusto
plug in - enchufar
pocket - bolsillo
pocketwatch - reloj de bolsillo
poet - poeta
poetry - poesía
point - punto
police station - estación de policías
polite - cortés
political analyst - analista político
political science - ciencias políticas
polyester - poliéster
poor - pobre
popcorn - palomitas
popular destinations - destinos populares
popular opinion - opinión popular
population - población
pork - puerco
posh - elegante
post office - oficina postal
pot - olla
potato - papa
power - poder
pragmatic - pragmático/a
praise - elogiar
prank - broma
prankster - bromista
pray - rezo
pre-nuptial agreement - acuerdo prenupcial
predict - predecir
prefer - preferir
pregnant - embarazada
prepaid card - tarjeta de prepago
preparation - preparación
preschoolers - preescolares
president - presidente
pressure - presión
pretty - bonito/a
prevent - evitar/impedir
previous - anterior
price - precio
pride - orgullo
priest - sacerdote
primero - first
principled - de principios

privacy - privacidad
problem - problema
process my mail - procesar mi correo
profession - profesión
professional - profesional
progeny - descendientes
promise - promesa
pronunciation - pronunciación
prophet - profeta
proposal - propuesta de matrimonio
prosperity - prosperidad
protein - proteína
province - provincia
proximity - proximidad
public transportation - transporte público
pulse - pulso
puncture - perforación
punishment - castigo
pupil - alumno/a
purple - morado
not on purpose - no fue a propósito
purse - cartera

Q

quality - calidad
quarter - cuarto
quarter past 10 - diez y cuarto
quarter to 11 - cuarta para las once
question - pregunta
quick witted - agudo/a
quickly - rápidamente
quiet - silencioso
quite a while ago - hace bastante tiempo
quitting - renunciar

R

radiant - radiante
to rain - llover
rain boots - botas de lluvia
raincoat - impermeable
raining day - día lluvioso
raisins - pasas
rashes - Erupciones
ratio - proporción
raw - crudo
raw vegetables - verduras crudas
to read - leer
I read - Leo
ready - listo/a
receipt - recibo
receive - recibir
reception - recepción
recommend - recomendar
you recommend - recomiendas
red - roja
refrigerator - refrigerador
my regards - mis saludos
region - región
regret - lamentar
rejection - rechazo
relatives - parientes
relax - relajar
religion - religión
remember - acordar
rent - rentar
rent a car - rentar auto

can you repeat - puedes repetir
repeat - repetir
request - solicitar
request (n) - solicitud
research - investigación
resemblance - semejanza
resent - resentir
resentment - rencor
reservation - reservación
reset meter - reiniciar el motor
respectful - respetuoso/a
responsibility - responsabilidad
responsible - responsable
rest - descanso
restaurant - restaurante
restaurants - restaurantes
retired - retirado
return - devolver
return the keys - devolver las llaves
reunion - reunión
review - reseña
reviews - críticas
rich - rico
right - derecha
right now - ahora mismo
rights - derechos
ring - anillo
river - río
road - carretera
road trip - viaje en carretera
road work - trabajo en la carretera
roast - asado
role model - modelo a seguir
roof - techo
room - habitación
room charges - cargas de habitación
room service - servicio de cuarto
rough - áspero
route - ruta
rude - grosero/a
rules - reglas
run - correr
running nose - nariz que moquea
rush hour - hora pico

S

sad - triste
safety - seguridad
saint - santo/a
salad - ensalada
salary - salario
sale - venta
sales tax - impuesto de venta
saliva - saliva
salt - sal
salty - salado
same - mismo
sand - arena
sandals - sandalias
Saturday - sábado
sausage - salchicha
savings - ahorros
to say - decir
scam - estafa
scanning machine - maquina de escaneo
scared - espantado/a
scarf - bufanda

scary - espantoso
scenery - escenario
school - escuela
school bag - bolsa escolar
schoolmates - compañeros de escuela
science - ciencias
scold - regañar
scooter - escúter
scream - gritar
scrutinize - escudriñar
seafood - mariscos
search - buscar
seasonal flu - gripe estacional
seasons - estaciones
second - segundo
secret recipe - Receta secreta
section - sección
security check - revisión de seguridad
sedan - sedán
to see - ver
self-reliant - autosuficiente
self-respect - respeto a si mismo
sell - vender
send - mandar
send email - enviar correo electrónico
send him - enviarle
send message - mandar mensaje
senior - mayor
sentiments - sentimientos
separate beds - camas separadas
separated - separado
September - septiembre
serious - serio/a
service - servicio
service fee - tarifa de servicio
to set - fijar
seven - siete
seventy - setenta
sewing - cocer
shade - sombra
shake hands - darse las manos
share - compartir
share the ride - compartir el viaje
shave - rasurar
she - Ella
shenanigan - shenanigan
shift - turno
shining - brillando
shiny - brilloso
shirt - camisa
shoe box - caja de zapatos
shoe shop - zapatería
shoes - zapatos
shopping - compras
shopping bag - bolsa de la compra
shopping center - centro comercial
short (in stature) - baja
short hair - cabello corto
short stay - estancia corta
short-lived - corta vida
shorts - shorts
should - deber
shoulders - hombros
show your face - enseñar tu

cara
shower - ducha
shower curtain - cortina de la ducha
shred - desgarrar
shrewd - perspicaz
shrink - encogimiento
shut off - apagar
sick - enfermo
sideburns - patillas
signs - señales
silver - plateado
silverware - cubiertos
similar - parecido
similarities - similitudes
sincere - sincero/a
sing - cantar
singing - cantando
single bed - cama individual
single layered - una sola capa
sink - lavabo
sister - hermana
sister-in-law - cuñada
to sit - sentar
six - seis
size - talla
skin - piel
sky - cielo
sleep - dormir
sleepy - soñoliento
sleeves - mangas
slice - rebanar
slim - delgado
slippery - resbaloso
slow - despacio
slow down - reducir velocidad
slowly - pausadamente
smack - golpe
small - pequeño
smell - olor
smile - sonrisa
smoking - de fumar
snow - nieve
snowfall - nevada
so-so - mas o menos
soak - empapar
soap - jabón
social media - medios de comunicación social
social order - orden social
social worker - trabajador social
socialism - socialismo
socialist - socialista
society - sociedad
socks - calcetines
soda - soda
soft - suave
Soltero - single
some other time - algún otra vez
something - algo
sometimes - a veces
son - hijo
son-in-law - yerno
song - canción
soon - pronto
sore throat - dolor de garganta
sound - sonido
it sounds - Suena
soup - sopa
sour - agrio
south America - Sudamérica

span - lapso
spare change - cambio suelto
sparkling water - agua carbonada
speak - hablar/platicar
speak slowly - habla despacio
speakers - altavoces
special moments - momentos especiales
speciality - especialidad
specialty shops - tiendas de especialidad
speed limit - límite de velocidad
spelling - ortografía
spices - especies
spicy - picante
spinach - espinaca
spiritual - espiritual
spoiled - mimado/a
spoon - cuchara
sport shoes - zapatos deportivos
sports - deportes
sports car - coche deportivo
sports jacket - chaqueta deportiva
spring - primavera
spring break - vacaciones de primavera
stairs - escaleras
stakes - estacas
start - empezar
starving - muriendo de hambre
state - estado
steak - bistec
steam - vapor
steamed - al vapor
steps - pasos
stimulate - estimular
stir - remover
stoic - estoico/a
stomach - estómago
stool - taburete
stop - detener
stop-over - pernoctar
store - tienda
storm - tormenta
story - historia
straight - derecho
straight hair - cabello lacio
stranger - desconocido/a
strap - correa/tira
strapped - amarrado/a
straw - popote
straw hat - sombrero de paja
street - calle
street food - comida de calle
strength - fuerza
stress - estrés
stressed - estresado/a
stretch - tramo
stripes - rayas
stroll - paseo
stroller - carriola
strong - fuerte
strong body - cuerpo fuerte
strong bond - lazo fuerte
struggle - luchar
stubborn - obstinado/a
student - estudiante
studying - estudiando
stupid - estúpido/a

subsidized - subvencionado
subtract - restar
subway - metro
suddenly - de repente
suffering - sufrimiento
sugar - azúcar
suit - traje
summer - verano
summer break - vacaciones de verano
sun - sol
Sunday - domingo
sunglasses - gafas del sol
sunny - soleado
sunny day - día soleado
sunrise - la salida del sol
sunset - atardecer
sunshine - la luz del sol
super - súper
supermarket - supermercado
supply - suministro
support - apoyo
surgery - cirugía
surprise - sorpresa
survival tips - tipos de supervivencia
swallow - tragar
swamped - inundado
sweat - sudor
sweater - suéter
sweet tooth - goloso
sweets - caramelos
swim - nadar
swimming pool - piscina
swimsuit - traje de baño
swing - columpio
sympathetic - simpático
synagogue - sinagoga

T

t-shirt - camiseta
table - mesa
table cloth - mantel
Taiwan dollar - dólar taiwanés
to take out - sacar
take - tomar
I take - Tomo
take a leave - tomar descanso
take a sip - sorber
take it - Tómalo
take me to - llévame al
take off - despegar
talk - hablar
I talk - Hablo
talkative - hablador/a
tall - alto
task - quehacer/tarea
taste - probar
tasty - sabroso
taxi - taxi
tea - té
teacher - maestro/a
team - equipo
tears - lagrimas
teary - lloroso
teenager - adolescente
television - televisión
teller - cajero/escrutador/a
temperature - temperatura
temple - templo
ten - diez
tenderness - ternura
tent - tienda de campaña

term - término
terrible - terrible
to thank - agradecer
thank you - Gracias
thank you very much - muchas gracias
thankful - agradecido/a
thanksgiving - día de acción de gracias
that - Ese
that - Eso
the - el
the - la
the - las
the - los
theater - teatro
theft - robo
Their - de ellos
their - su
them - ellos
then - luego
there are - Hay
there is - Hay
thick - grueso
thighs - muslos
thin - flaco
think - pensar
third - Tercero
thirst - sed
this (f) - ésta
this (m) - éste
this (neuter) - esto
those - esos
thoughtful - considerado/atento
thoughts - pensamientos
thread - hilo
three - tres
thumb - pulgar
Thursday - jueves
ticket - boleto
tickets - boletos
tickle - hacer cosquillas
tight - apretado
time/hour - hora
time - tiempo
time zone - zona horaria
timely - oportuno
tip - propina
tire - llanta
tired - cansado/a
to - a
to the - al
toes - dedos del pie
together - juntos
the toilet - el excusado
toilet paper - papel higiénico
tolerate - tolerar
tomato - tomate
tomorrow - mañana
day after tomorrow - pasado mañana
tongue - lengua
tonsils - amígdalas
toothbrush - cepillo de dientes
toothpaste - pasta de dientes
top floor - ultimo piso
torch - linterna
tornado - tornado
tourism - turismo
tourists - turistas
towel - toalla
town - municipio
toys - juguetes
tradition - tradición

traditional - tradicional
traditional healers - curanderos tradicionales
traditional medicine - medicina tradicional
traditional stores - tiendas tradicionales
traffic - tráfico
traffic signal - señal de tráfico
train - tren
tranquil - tranquilo
transaction - transacción
trash - basura/desperdicio
to travel - viajar
travel agent - agente de viaje
travel buddies - compañeros de viaje
travellers - viajeros
treatment - tratamiento
trees - arboles
trend - tendencia
tres veces - thrice
tribe - tribu
trick - truco
trim - recortar
trip - viaje
triple - triple
tropical - tropical
truck - camión
true story - historia verdadera
Tuesday - martes
turkey - pavo
Turkish - turco
turn - virar
turn off - apagar
turn on - prender
twenty - veinte
twilight - crepúsculo
twin - gemelo/a
two - dos
two-story - dos pisos

U

ugly - feo
umbrella - paraguas
una vez - once
unable to walk - incapaz de caminar
unbelievable - increíble
uncle - tío
unconditional love - amor incondicional
under-cooked - medio crudo
under-weight - bajo peso
undergrad - licenciatura
understand - entiendo
underwear - calzones
underweight - bajo peso
unemployed - desempleado
unexpected - inesperado/a
unfair - injusto
unfold - desplegar
unhappy - infeliz
uniform - uniforme
united - unido
university - universidad
unlock - abrir cerradura
unlucky - desafortunado
unmarried - soltero/a
unpack - desempacar
unpopular - impopular
until - hasta
unwell - indispuesto

up - arriba
upscale - de lujo
upset - trastornado
urine - orina
use - utilizar
useful - útil
useful tips - consejos útiles
I utilize - Utilizo

V

value added tax - impuesta al valor agregado
values - valores
vegetable soup - sopa de verduras
vegetables - verduras
vegetarian - vegetariano
Venezuelan - venezolana
verify - verificar
vertigo - vértigo
very good - muy bueno
very large - muy grande
very small - muy pequeño
vice-president - vicepresidente
view - mirar
vilify - vilipendiar
village - pueblo
visa stamp - sello de visa
to visit - visitar
I visited - Visité
visit visa - visa de extranjero
vote - voto
vows - juramentos

W

waist line - cintura
wait - esperar
wait time - tiempo de espera
waiter - mesero
waiting - esperando
wake up - despierto
walk - caminar
wallet - billetera
I want - Quiero
want to - querer
warm - cálido
was - fue
to wash - lavar
I wash - Lavo
waste bin - canasta de basura
wasteful spending - gasto inútil
I watch - Veo
water - agua
water heater - calentador de agua
watermelon - sandía
we - Nosotros
weak - débil
weak eyesight - mala vista
wealth - riqueza
weather - clima
wedding - boda
wedding dress - vestido de novia
wedding party - fiesta de bodas
wedding photo - foto de boda
Wednesday - miércoles
week - semana
weight - peso
weight limit - límite de peso
welcome - bienvenida

well - bien
well-being - bienestar
well-dressed - bien vestido
well-groomed - bien arreglado
well-mannered - bien portado/a
well-nourished - bien nutrido
well-spoken - bien hablado
well-trained - bien entrenado
well-written - bien escrito
west Asia - Asia del oeste
wet - mojado
what - cuál
what - cuales
what - qué
wheel - rueda
wheelchair - silla de ruedas
when - cuándo
where - dónde
Whether - ya sea
which - cuál
which - qué
whisper - susurrar
whistle - silbar
white - blanco
who - quien
whole wheat - integral
whom - quien
whose - de quien
why - porqué
wide chest - pecho ancho
widowed - viudo/a
wife - esposa
wild - silvestre
wilderness - yermo
I will - Voy
willpower - fuerza de voluntad
wind - viento
windbreaker - rompevientos
window seat - asiento de la ventana
windows - ventanas
wine - vino
wing-span - envergadura
wings - alas
winter - invierno
winter break - vacaciones de invierno
wipe - limpiar
wire - cable
wisdom - sabiduría
wise - sabio/a
wish - deseo
with - con
with family - con familia
with pleasure - con placer
with you - contigo
withdraw - retirar
without - sin
woman - mujer
wool - lana
word of honor - palabra de honor
to work - trabajar
you work - trabajas
work (n) - trabajo
work related - relacionado al trabajo
workers day - día de los trabajadores
world - mundo
worse - peor

worst - lo peor
would be - sería
wristband - pulsera
write - escribir
write a letter - escribir una carta

Y

yawn - bostezo
year - año
years - años
yellow - amarilla
yellow - amarillo
yes - sí
yesterday - ayer
you (formal) - usted
you (informal) - tú
young - joven
young at heart - joven de corazón
young ones - jóvenes
younger - menor
your - tu
youth - juventud

Z

zipper - cierre

www.ingramcontent.com/pod-product-compliance
Lightning Source LLC
Chambersburg PA
CBHW060011050426
42448CB00012B/2706

Contents...

THANK YOU...

Jesus Christ for the salvation you purchased with your life and offer freely to all who will believe and accept it.

Reverend Dalton Heath who shared the gospel with me and led me to Christ when I was eleven.

Reverend Ed Hargis (in heaven), my father in the ministry and my mentor.

Ahoskie Free Will Baptist Church for allowing me to be your pastor and helping me develop my approach to leading others to Jesus Christ.

Amy D. Harris for your love and support for this book and my entire ministry.

Sandy Atwood for your help in editing and making this book a better one.

Recommended by Others

Reverend Reuben Cason,

Promotional Director, North Carolina State Association of Free Will Baptists.

Whether a seasoned pastor or a new convert, if one will follow Dr. Harris' personal evangelism plan, many lost souls will be saved. ***When Angels Rejoice*** captures the essence of sharing the Gospel with confidence and simplicity. Every believer who is committed to obeying the Great Commission should read this book. But not just read it, put in to practice these time-tested suggestions on how to lead someone to faith in Christ. Dr. Roy Harris has not only preached these principles, he has practiced them at home and abroad. And now, we can learn from his years of personal evangelism experience as we seek to win lost souls to Christ. Jesus said, *"the harvest truly is great, but the laborers are few" (*Luke 10:2), but if we put into practice this model of personal evangelism, we will *"doubtless come again with rejoicing, bringing our sheaves with us"* (Psalm 126:6).

8

Randy Evans - The first person Roy trained in personal evangelism is a *layman* and teaches Biotechnology at Grantham Middle School in Goldsboro, NC. He and his wife Katrina attend Faith Free Will Baptist Church in Goldsboro, NC.

In the early 1980's Roy Harris became my pastor and friend. My wife and I began attending his church in Ahoskie, NC. Roy taught us the importance of personal soul winning and the crucial role of church members in this process. After training and role-playing, Roy asked me to go out with him to share Christ with others. He helped me put the personal soul winning knowledge I'd learned into practice. He made it so clear and simple; it was fun, rewarding and exciting to share Christ with others. We saw several souls saved and our church began to flourish with new Christians and all the excitement that comes with seeing people come to Christ. This book, *When Angels Rejoice* puts in written form what Roy taught us. I know he loves souls and God is using his ministry throughout the world, bringing many souls to Christ.

Reverend Richard Atwood, *Church Planter*, former *Director of Missionary Assistance* for North American Missions and presently pastors *Truth and Grace Church*, a new mission church in Mount Juliet, Tennessee.

I am glad to recommend this book from a man that I know is the real deal. I see this book as being greatly used in training church groups – Sunday School, Small groups, Midweek meetings. Here are a couple of great quotes from the book:

"*We must look at the world through eternal eyes.*"

"*Time is a precious personal commodity! Personal evangelism requires an investment of time.*"

"*Remember, our job is not to save anyone. We are seed sowers.*"

"*The best hope for our world today is the engagement of us Christians, one-on-one with the world around us, sharing our faith in Jesus Christ.*"

Impact in East Africa

Bishop Chris Barasa Luswetti pastors in **Eldoret, Kenya** and is overseer of *Word of Life Harvest Church Ministries of East Africa* including ministries in *Kenya, Uganda, Rwanda, Burundi* and *The Republic of Congo*. God used this man to open the door for Roy's Ministry in East Africa.

God connected us with Dr. Roy Harris in a unique way. Dr. Roy has invested so much in our pastors and leaders. The seeds he planted continue to grow and we've seen great changes in the lives of our pastors and church leaders. His skills in the ministry have changed the way our leaders think and do things. They are putting what they received into practice and we are experiencing a great harvest of souls. Dr. Roy continues to mentor me, and my group of leaders. We in turn are mentoring hundreds in our cities and communities. He has trained a large number of pastors in Kenya, Uganda, Tanzania, Rwanda and Burundi. We have recently spread his teachings to The

Republic of Congo. We've seen many new healthy churches planted. Since Dr. Roy came to Africa over five years ago, we've held several crusades putting into practice his evangelistic message. Through his training and preaching we've seen many souls give their lives to Jesus in our communities and cities. Our churches have grown spiritually and also in numbers. His books have helped and empowered many pastors. Dr. Roy's latest book; ***When Angels Rejoice*** *will be a great tool for our pastors and leaders in sharing the gospel through personal evangelism. Let us pray for this man of God who has a big heart for our pastors and church leaders in Africa. Pray that the Lord may add to him many days and that Dr. Roy will live a long life so that he can continue to equip and empower more pastors.*

Introduction

The thought of talking with others about their spiritual condition and eternal destiny may evoke feelings of inadequacy, lack of confidence, and sometimes just plain fear.

Most people have a love and concern for others. They see the devastation and unhappiness in the lives of others and know that Christ is the only answer. They would like to share their faith and introduce others to the wonderful life they've found through the Lord Jesus Christ, but they do not know how.

The two greatest obstacles in sharing one's faith are lack of knowledge and fear. Not knowing how to begin a conversation on spiritual things and how to move the conversation towards the most important questions in life stop many people before they begin. Not being sure what to say garners fear and paralyzes individuals when it comes to sharing their faith. The purpose in penning the words that follow is to provide tools to help anyone who desires to lead others to Christ. The following pages contain a practical, simple, and effective way to approach loved ones and friends in sharing one's faith. The knowledge that may be gained is derived from 35 years of personal experience in personally leading others to Christ, and has been taught to countless individuals in America and around the world.

This book attempts to accomplish six things:

1. Develop a *sense of urgency* for reaching people who do not know Christ with the Gospel.
2. Determine *the tools necessary* to be effective in personal evangelism.
3. Develop *the skills needed* to bring others to a saving knowledge of Jesus Christ.

4. Develop *confidence in approaching others* and presenting the Good News of Jesus Christ.
5. Develop *awareness of those around us* who do not know Christ.
6. Develop *a plan for training others* to become involved in personal evangelism.

The principles suggested in this book are not merely theory, but were forged in the trenches of one-on-one encounters in personally leading countless people to Christ.

This book can be a valuable resource for individuals, pastors and Christian leaders to become more effective soul winners. The book can also be used as a great training tool to equip others in becoming effective in reaching people with the Gospel.

The *Gospel* or *Good News* is the same in every culture and country because Jesus Christ is the same yesterday, today and forever (Hebrews 13:8). The method may be modified, but the principles of personal evangelism contained in this book can be effective in most any country or culture.

It is my prayer that the approach and common sense principles found in this book will revolutionize the reader and result in untold multitudes coming to a saving knowledge of Jesus Christ.

YOU CAN BE AN EFFECTIVE SOUL WINNER!

Chapter 1

Beginning the Journey

I unpacked my books and organized my office, settling into my first pastorate in the small town of Ahoskie, North Carolina. My desire to be a pastor had led me away from a faculty position as Dean of Men at Welch College in Nashville, Tennessee to this new chapter in my life.

I didn't know what the future might hold, but I recognized quickly that I must set the example and be out front leading my people in any direction I asked them to go. I also realized that if our church was to grow, then I must chart a clear course and a simple path for my congregation to follow.

The most important task that lay ahead of me was communicating the Good News of Jesus Christ to those who were without hope in my sphere of influence.

I sat under Mr. Ralph Hampton's Personal Evangelism course during my freshman year at Welch College. Scripture memorization was a vital part of that course. We had to memorize over

150 Scripture verses from the Bible. But I'm sorry to say; I did not see then how important that course would be later in life.

I quickly realized that if our church was to grow, the most important thing I could do was to become burdened for the unsaved in our community. I began to pray and ask the Lord to make me sensitive and aware of the unsaved people around me.

With this new sense of awareness came a desire to bring these people to Christ. How? It became obvious that I needed to become more effective in talking with people one-on-one about their spiritual conditions.

The Bible verses I memorized became the bedrock on which I developed an approach to discussing eternal matters resulting in giving people hope.

I began by consulting pastor friends on how they approached this serious matter. I visited bookstores and tried to become knowledgeable of the resources that were available on the subject. I purchased and intently read a number of those resources.

I asked the Lord to help me glean from these resources principles and approaches, which might help me in developing my own approach. In a few weeks a simple outline was formed and an approach developed.

For the past 35 years my approach has undergone minor adjustments in order to adapt to the cultural changes that have occurred over these past 35 years, but has remained basically the same.

Those early days began with a trial and error effort. Each time I talked with individuals one-on-one, my confidence grew as I watched the power of Scripture and the convicting presence of the Holy Spirit change the lives of many people. I became convinced that the message I was sharing was changing lives.

Decades have passed and many souls have entered God's kingdom through the gospel shared in this one-on-one approach to personal evangelism.

The approach developed back in the early days has been shared many times in a variety of venues. I personally trained individuals in the four full-time churches I pastored, a generation of young champions for Christ at Welch College, a variety of evangelism conferences across America, and pastors and church leaders in Kenya, Uganda, and Tanzania.

Personal evangelism training

received by pastors and leaders in East Africa has resulted in literally hundreds of souls coming to Christ. Over 100 new churches have been started in East Africa.

It has been said *the longest journey begins with a single step*. This book can become your first *small step* beginning a new *big journey* of sharing your faith with friends and family whom you may care for deeply.

Lack of knowledge and fear are the greatest obstacles that keep people from sharing their faith. This book can help you obtain the knowledge, overcome your fear, and gain confidence enabling you to lead others to a saving knowledge of Jesus Christ.

Congratulations, you have begun your journey. Please read carefully the words written in this book. You are unique. Take the approach shared in this book and let it be a guide for you as you *develop your own approach* to sharing the path of salvation with others.

Remember, it is not your responsibility to save anyone. Your responsibility is to share the good news that Jesus Christ provides salvation to all who will trust Him. More will be said later in the book, but at this point the important thing is to take your first step in beginning your journey in personal evangelism.

Let me encourage you to consider learning the verses found throughout the book. Remember the Bible in Romans 10:37 says *truth comes by hearing, and hearing by the word of God.*

Pray for the Lord to make you more aware of unsaved people around you and to burden your heart for their eternal destinies. Ask the Lord to place someone on your heart to pray for and also to open a door of opportunity to share your faith with others.

Chapter 2

What is Personal Evangelism?

Preliminary Considerations

The voice on the other end of the phone was one I knew well. Many years had passed since I'd had the privilege of pastoring the church in which he still was serving as a deacon.

His voice was trembling and I sensed the news he was about to share would not be good. *Preacher Harris, I have some bad news* he said.

I replied by asking what had happened? He began to share the details of a tragic event that had taken place with one of the church families. You'll never guess what he shared with me and I'll tell you at the end of this chapter.

There are some preliminary considerations that we should examine in defining personal evangelism. Let's begin by examining both words.

Personal, in conjunction with the

word *evangelism*, suggests a number of things.

First, when we think of *personal* in personal evangelism, the idea of a *face-to-face encounter* comes to mind. One-on-one interaction is required.

Second, because this is personal, upfront, and requires a close encounter, this type of evangelism places the individual in a *vulnerable position*. When you talk to someone face-to-face, the reality of the situation becomes very clear. You can see the person's demeanor and he can read your sincerity.

You've asked permission to enter

their private space. By doing so, you also granted them entrance into your personal space as well.

Third, this one-on-one encounter is the most effective way to reach people for Christ. Our Lord used this approach when calling many people to follow Him. By talking with individuals personally, one lends himself to the nudging and guiding of the Holy Spirit.

The Primary Command

Preach the Word!

I discovered a great definition of evangelism many years ago and I'm sorry that I can't recall the source. This is not my definition but I think it's a great one. *Evangelism* is the spreading of the Christian Gospel by public preaching or personal witness.

The apostle Paul instructed young Timothy in 1 Timothy 4:2 to *preach the word; be ready in season and out of season; reprove, rebuke, and exhort, with complete patience and teaching* (ESV).

There are two words in the Greek New Testament that are translated preach.

In Acts 8:4 the Greek word *κηρύττω* *(kirýtto)* is used. This word could be better translated as evangelize or deliver the Good News of the Gospel to individuals one-on-one. This word clearly describes that *personal evangelism* is one form of *preaching the word*.

In Acts 8:5 the Greek word *κηρύττουν (kirýttoun)* is used. This word, in the context of the passage, is announcing the Good News of the Gospel to a crowd or more than one individual.

The apostle Paul was a shining example of both ways of preaching. When entering a city he usually went to the local synagogue to proclaim the gospel of Jesus Christ to the Jewish population first.

He would do this in a public setting using the Old Testament Scriptures along with the declaration of the divinity of Jesus Christ.

Paul also approached many people face-to-face on an individual basis. There are many examples in the New Testament. The important thing to remember is that we are instructed to do both. Unfortunately, with the rise of full-time pastors and paid church staff, we have relegated the responsibility of winning others to Christ to them and removed it from individual church members.

The Bible makes it clear that every Christian has a responsibility to share his or her faith as the Holy Spirit provides opportunity and gives direction to them. The gospel was spread around the world because of individuals continually confronting others face-to-face with the hope the gospel offers. We understand the power of the pulpit, but we must also remember the power in the pew. Full-time staff members are few when compared to the number of individual church members in each congregation.

We must become a force of individuals seeking to bring others to a saving knowledge of Jesus Christ. We should stop and remember that we are fortunate. We have hope and purpose in life. We have that hope and purpose because someone cared enough for us to share the gospel.

We have a responsibility to share the gospel, which is not a choice, according to Scriptures. We must be actively concerned about the spiritual condition of those around us.

We should also remember the hope for the future does not lie in political parties. Hope lies in the gospel of Jesus Christ.

The Personalities Involved

There are four entities that are necessary in order for personal evangelization to be successful. Each one plays a unique role. God chose this approach.

Christians *communicate* the gospel to the unsaved. The role of Christians is not to save anyone because that is not possible. But they are to share the gospel with individuals who do not know Christ as their Savior.

The Christian role is vital in the evangelization of the unsaved world. God selected Christians and bestowed upon them the great honor of carrying the most important message the world has ever known.

The ***Holy Spirit*** *convicts* those who do not know Christ and makes them aware of their lost condition before God.

The Holy Spirit places the heavy realization of the burden of sin and the transgression of God's standards of righteousness, squarely on the shoulders of the unsaved.

The unsaved must feel convicted of their sins and recognize they are lost and alienated from God before they will become ready to receive the gospel message. The Holy Spirit is the convicting force that helps the unsaved understand and come to grips with their lost condition.

The ***Gospel*** *convinces* the unsaved that salvation is available through faith in Jesus Christ. Don't underestimate the power of the Scriptures in convincing the unsaved person that there is hope for them because of what Christ did on the cross of Calvary. Romans 10:17 reminds us that *Faith comes from hearing, and hearing through the word of God* (ESV).

The ***Unsaved*** *commits* to the gospel message. After the Christian communicates the gospel and the unsaved person has a clear understanding of the message, the Holy Spirit convicts the unsaved person, helps them to realize their lost condition, and the gospel convinces the unsaved person that there is hope through faith in Jesus Christ. The decision to accept or reject this wonderful gift is left totally to the free will of the unsaved person.

All four entities play a vital role in the transformation from spiritual death into eternal life.

Now, back to the phone call.

Preacher Harris, I have some bad news. I'm sure you remember Ken ______. He's been killed in a horrible accident.

He began to give the details of what happened. Ken worked at a timber processing plant and operated a machine that stripped bark away from logs. A log jammed in the machine. He stepped down from the cab and tried to free the jammed log.

The unthinkable happened! The log slipped free when Ken pried it loose and the machine pulled it into the stripper. Ken was wearing a heavy winter coat and the machine grippers grabbed the bottom of his coat. Ken was pulled into the sharp stripper blades and in an instant he was cut into pieces from the waist up.

My heart sank and I immediately thought of his wife and children. Then my thoughts went to memories of Ken. I had the privilege of leading him and his wife to Christ a dozen years earlier. I also baptized him, his wife and two sons. The split second Ken left this world; he entered a world without pain or death. He was in Christ's presence.

The urgency of personally sharing our faith in Christ cannot be over emphasized. I asked God to help me learn to share my faith with others and He did. I shared with Ken how he could know for sure that if he died he could be with Christ in heaven. He's in heaven today!

Chapter 3

Why is Personal Evangelism Important?

Theological Reasons

Daktari Roy, do you have time to talk with me? I met John O. on my second trip to Kenya in 2013. I preached and taught at a pastors and church leaders conference he'd planned and organized in Kisumu, Kenya on the shores of Lake Victoria in East Africa.

I spoke 16 times in 5 days and focused on training pastors and church leaders on the importance of and 'how to' of personal evangelism. Over 300 Africans from several denominations and tribes attended the conference.

I sensed that Pastor John's focus was more on orphanages than evangelism and pastoral training. Boy was I mistaken!

It was 2016 and I hadn't seen John in almost three years. We sat down in the lobby of my hotel Le Savanna Hotel in Kisumu and he began to tell me a story that was exciting and almost unbelievable.

I will recount this exciting story at the end of this chapter.

Christ is the **ONLY MEANS** of salvation for everyone. Acts 4:12 makes it clear that *there is salvation in no one else, for there is no other name under heaven given among men by which we must be saved*.

This statement is a reminder of Jesus' declaration in John 14:6 that He is *the way, the truth, the life and if anyone is to have access to God the father, that access can come only through Him*. There is no other way! Jesus is the only means of salvation and He is available to every person around the world.

God **CHOSE THIS METHOD** to reach the world. When Jesus ascended back to heaven after his resurrection, he left specific instructions to his followers. He gave them specific instructions on how others would learn about Him.

In Acts 1:8, Jesus said *you will receive power when the Holy Spirit has come upon you, and you will be my witnesses in Jerusalem and in all Judea and Samaria, and to the end of the earth.*

Those instructions resulted in the spreading of the gospel around the world. This God chosen method has remained unchanged for over 2000 years.

Personal Evangelism is the **BEST HOPE** for our MODERN WORLD. In Ephesians 2:14-22 Paul tells us that *Jesus is our peace, who made both groups into one and broke down the barrier of the dividing wall, by abolishing in His flesh the enmity, which is the Law of commandments contained in ordinances, so that in Himself He might make the two into one new man, thus establishing peace, and might reconcile them both in one body to God through the cross, by it having put to death the enmity. AND HE CAME AND PREACHED PEACE TO YOU WHO WERE FAR AWAY,*

AND PEACE TO THOSE WHO WERE NEAR; for through Him we both have our access in one Spirit to the Father.

So then you are no longer strangers and aliens, but you are fellow citizens with the saints, and are of God's household, having been built on the foundation of the apostles and prophets, Christ Jesus Himself being the corner stone, in whom the whole building, being fitted together, is growing into a holy temple in the Lord, in whom you also are being built together into a dwelling of God in the Spirit.

The world is seeking personal, community, national and international peace. The best hope for our world is the peace offered through Jesus Christ.

Peace can only be found when one is at peace with himself. The only way we can find true inner peace is when we have peace with God. Since the only means of salvation is through Jesus Christ, then peace with God may only be found through faith in His Son.

The best hope for our world today is the engagement of Christians, one-on-one with the world around us sharing our faith in Jesus Christ. Personal evangelism is by far the best hope for our modern world.

Ethical Reasons

Christ showed us compassion; we must show that same compassion to others. Matthew 9:36-38 tells us when Jesus saw the crowds, *he had compassion for them, because they were harassed and helpless, like sheep without a shepherd. Then He said to his disciples, the harvest is plentiful, but the laborers are few; therefore pray earnestly to the Lord of the harvest to send out laborers into his harvest.*

Someone cared enough to share the good news of salvation through Jesus Christ with us. Christ's compassion was extended to us through them. Therefore, we should share that same compassion with others.

It would be selfish on our part to hide the wonderful light received and fail to give its glow to others.

Sharing the gospel is the right thing to do. In Mark 16:15, Jesus instructs us to *go all over the world and share the gospel with everyone*. This is not a request by Jesus. This is a command. We are to *go and proclaim* the gospel to the whole creation.

Practical Reasons

Some people can only be reached through *personal evangelism*. They will not attend church and their main contact with Christ will come through interaction with those who have Christ in their lives.

The only hope they have for salvation is the obedience of believers who are prompted by the Holy Spirit to share the Gospel with them. This places a high level of responsibility and urgency on the shoulders of believers.

Other methods of evangelism such as event evangelism, neighborhood outreach, street evangelism, evangelistic crusades and relational evangelism swing on the hinge of personal evangelism. The one-to-one interaction of personal evangelism is necessary at some point regardless of the approach to evangelization.

It has been proven that churches that fail to become involved in personal evangelism <u>will die in two generations</u>.

I was not sure what Pastor John wanted to say to me. He'd since connected with another pastor from Oklahoma and I had connected with a totally new group in Kisumu since our time together three years ago.

John began by thanking me for coming to Kisumu in 2013. He told me a story that made my heart rejoice and also excited my spirit. He said *Do you remember teaching how to lead others to Jesus Christ? Well, God has done a great work since you were here.*

I asked him what God had done. He began to give details of God's miraculous hand and a replication of the New Testament model of personal evangelism.

He said *Daktari Roy, when you were here in 2013, we had 14 churches in Kisumu and the adjoining regions. We now have 40 churches.*

I wanted to make sure I'd understood correctly what he'd just said. So I said *26 new churches have begun in less than three years?* He responded that 26 new churches had begun in less than three years.

I asked him what were the key factors to such phenomenal growth in churches. Personal evangelism! He told me that the pastors and leaders had put into practice the training they'd received in how to lead others to Christ.

Their approach was to go into villages, communities and cities and talk with people one-on-one and share the good news of the gospel. They would win them and others to Christ and begin a new church. This had been done at least 26 times in less than three years.

He also told me that these pastors were replicating the training they'd received with others who in turn were also becoming soul winners.

He told me that he personally had been and was continuing to train young pastors on a weekly basis how to share the gospel and win others to Christ.

Personal evangelism works!

Chapter 4

Let's Get Started

A Saturday morning meeting was scheduled and I arrived at the church early. I walked from my office through the educational building to the rest room and was alarmed to find the lower half of a man's torso on the floor in the open doorway of the restroom.

I was relieved when the body moved. Elmer was the kind of person every pastor loves to have around. He arrived early to repair a problem with the men's restroom sink. That was Elmer.

Elmer was an alcoholic and a rough man before becoming a Christian. His salvation experience was transforming and he became a completely changed man. He was a kind, gentle man of character who mowed the church lawn, served as Sunday School superintendent and church trustee and one of the all around good guys.

Fast forward to our spring revival services. Dr. Joe Ange, campus pastor from Welch College, was our guest speaker. Elmer came forward during the invitation in our first service on Sunday morning. I knelt down beside him and asked him why he'd come forward? You'll never guess why he came and what he said. At the end of this chapter, I'll tell you the rest of the story.

Let's begin our journey towards winning others to Christ. There are a number of steps one should take.

Catch the Vision

First, we must look at the world through eternal eyes. Personal evangelism is a matter of life and death. We should remember the eternal destiny of heaven or hell for friends, coworkers, neighbors and family members is at stake.

We must see people as God sees them, without hope and in need of help. We must believe that the answer to their problems is salvation through Jesus Christ. We should clearly understand that *where there is no vision the people will perish* Proverbs 29:18.

Ask the Lord to help you see people as He sees them. Pray and ask Him to give you a burden for the unsaved around you.

Commit to the Task

In Matthew 5:14-16 Jesus gives an illustration of what a candle does and He reminds us that the candle's purpose is to give light.

Modern parallel to that illustration would be a bright light in the dark room. The room remains pitch black without the presence of the light. But when the light enters the room the darkness disappears.

Jesus tells us that we are his light in this dark world. He instructs us to let our light shine brightly so that others will be drawn to Him because of that light which shines in us.

How do we do this? By committing ourselves to the task of personally sharing the good news of the gospel with others. Once we have made that commitment we can move forward with the task.

Conquer Fear

Psalms 34:4 tells us that *if we seek the Lord he will hear us and deliver us from our fears.* Many times fear comes because of the unknown. The lack of knowledge can generate feelings of fear.

You can conquer your fear with the Lord's help and also by applying yourself to gaining insight and knowledge from the material in this book. The approach taken will help you in a simple practical way learn how to lead people to a saving knowledge of Jesus Christ.

You can successfully conquer your fears!

Contact and Cultivate

Once you gain the knowledge that will help you conquer your fear and prepare you to share the gospel with others, you will be ready for the next step.

The next step will be following the leading of the Holy Spirit as he directs you to share the gospel with others. Interacting with others is essential in the spreading of the gospel through personal evangelism.

God will direct you to specific individuals with whom you will be able to share saving knowledge of the gospel.

The details of how to share the

gospel will be mentioned later in the book. But for now, remember that if you pray and ask the Lord to open doors of opportunity to share the gospel, he will do that and more.

Confront the Issue

The next step is helping individuals understand their lost condition and need of salvation offered through Jesus Christ. More will be said about this in a later chapter.

There are simple questions that may be asked, when answered, bring this important issue front and center. An easy to remember approach will be discussed in detail later in this book.

Now back to our story. I saw Elmer coming forward during the invitation. This is one of my best church members. Why would he be coming forward? I would soon learn why.

I knelt beside Elmer and placed my hand on his shoulder. I asked him why he came forward. He told me that he was concerned about his family and wanted to see them in church. He made a statement that I will remember the rest of my life.

Elmer said; *Preacher, I'd give my life to see my whole family in church.* He also came forward in the evening service and each of the next five services until revival services ended on Friday evening. His tears dripped from his face onto the altar and spilled onto the carpet. I knew Elmer meant what he'd said and he'd prayed fervently that God would do whatever was necessary to see his family in church and under the sound of the gospel.

The phone rang on Thursday morning and my secretary informed me that I had a call from our local hospital. The person on the line told me that Elmer was in the emergency room and the prognosis wasn't good.

I drove to the hospital and one of

the ER doctors met me at the door. Ahoskie, North Carolina is a small town and pastors hold a special respect among the people. The hospital personnel knew me well and appreciated the pastor's role and impact in our community.

He took a young summer intern minister from Welch College and me to a consultation room and told us that Elmer was dead. He had a massive heart attack in front of the hospital while stopped at a traffic light in his work truck.

The doctor led us to the treatment room where Elmer's lifeless body was lying. I thanked the Lord for Elmer and prayed for his family. I had the difficult task of leaving the hospital driving to Elmer's home to share the tragic news with his dear wife.

I was honored to preach his funeral on Saturday afternoon.

The next morning was the Lord's Day. I walked into the church auditorium between Sunday School and morning worship and was pleasantly surprised to see Elmer's entire family sitting on rows three and four on the right side.

I stepped to the pulpit determined to fulfill Elmer's wishes. I delivered a message of hope and a clear challenge to accept the free gift of salvation.

I relayed to his family what Elmer

shared with me 10 days before, with tears flowing down his face. I told them not only did Jesus die to make salvation available to everyone, but Elmer also offered to give his life for their opportunity to be in church and hear the gospel.

Chapter 5

Characteristics of Effective Soul Winners

The invitation to speak in a pastors and church leaders conference in Eldoret, Kenya was unexpected. I was honored when asked and humbly accepted the invitation.

What should I speak on? What would be the most beneficial to the African church leaders? What could help advance Christ's kingdom in East Africa? I prayed earnestly asking God to give me wisdom and guide me in the direction He would have me go.

God impressed to share with these leaders how they could become effective soul winners by engaging in personal evangelism. I began the step-by-step approach of how to personally become involved and how to share the plan of salvation with others.

The results were phenomenal and what God did was extraordinary. I'll share the details at the end of this chapter.

One can learn the necessary steps

and equip oneself with the best tools, but there are some characteristics that must be present if one is to be successful. I've listed nine below. More characteristics could be added to the list but here are some crucial ones.

1. Personal Assurance

One cannot convince others of what he is not sure of himself.

John 1:45 *Philip found Nathanael, and saith unto him, we have found him, of whom Moses in the law, and the prophets, did write, Jesus of Nazareth, the son of Joseph.*

We must know beyond doubt that we believe in the saving power of Jesus

Christ. We believe that Christ is who He said He was and did what He and others claimed He did. We will not be able to convince others unless we are totally convinced ourselves.

One can be strong in what he believes.

Daniel 1:10 *Now when Daniel knew that the writing was signed, he went into his house; and his windows being open in his chamber toward Jerusalem, he kneeled upon his knees three times a day, and prayed, and gave thanks before his God, as he did aforetime.*

It's possible to be totally convinced and be strong in the assurance that

Jesus has saved us. Strength will come from that belief and will help you stand firm on the faith that you have in Christ's saving power.

Assurance is based on God's Word.

1 John 5:13 *These things have I written unto you that believe on the name of the Son of God; that ye may know that ye have eternal life, and that ye may believe on the name of the Son of God.*

Our assurance is not based on emotions or momentary feelings. Occasionally these can and do change.

Our assurance is based on the Holy Scriptures, which is the inspired Word of God.

2. ***Personal Conviction***

Men and women are lost.

Romans 6:23 *For the reward of sin is death; but what God freely gives is eternal life in Jesus Christ our Lord.*

We must believe that men and women who do not accept Christ as Savior are doomed to eternal separation from God and endless torment in Hell. If we do not really believe they are doomed we have little incentive to try and reach them with the Gospel.

<u>Christ is the only hope for the Lost</u>.

John 3:18 *He that believeth on him is not condemned: but he that believeth not is condemned already, because he hath not believed in the name of the only begotten Son of God*.

The false hope of the world teaches that all roads (religions) lead to the one true God. He is simply called by other names and as long as you are sincere in what you believe you will be okay in the end.

Most of us have been sincere at times; only to find out we were wrong.

Those who place their hope and trust in anything but Jesus Christ will be condemned. They will be sincerely wrong but wrong none-the-less.

3. Personal Purity

Be Holy

1 Peter 1:15 but just as he who called you is holy, you yourselves also be holy in all of your behavior. (WEB)

A good definition of holy is: *to be dedicated and consecrated to God*. Holiness is a condition and not an act.

There is a genuine desire to be like Christ inside and out. The act of dedication requires a consecration, which evolves from a deep realization of who

God is.

Knowing who God is brings us face to face with our own personal sin and our unworthiness to be in His presence. We develop a deep appreciation for Christ whose holiness opens the door to the holiest of places to us, God's divine presence.

Becoming an effective soul-winner requires a clean vessel that can be used by the Holy Spirit. Clean vessels are holy vessels. This is not optional!

We are commanded to be holy. Why? Because we are vessels that carry the healing message of salvation to a world in desperate need of help and hope.

Abstain from all appearance of Evil.

1 Thessalonians 5:22 *Abstain from all appearance of evil. (KJV)* Holiness is an ongoing process. It will continue until we take our last breath on earth. Unholy living compromises holiness.

How? One example would be a clean cup or glass. Such a container can be used to hold many different things.

4. Personal Sacrifice

Crucifixion of Self

Galatians 2:*20 I have been put to death on the cross with Christ; still I am living; no longer I, but Christ is living in me; and that life which I now am living in the flesh I am living by faith, the faith of the Son of God, who in love for me, gave himself up for me.* (BBE) If one is to reach others for Christ it will require personal sacrifice.

In this verse, the apostle Paul makes the statement that the old Paul had died and the new Paul is alive forevermore through Christ Jesus. He makes the case that Christ made the supreme sacrifice when Christ gave himself for us and now lives in us and should control our actions.

Paul states in first Corinthians

15:31 that *personal sacrifice is a daily action of dying to ourselves.* This requires a continued battle between our fleshly side and our spiritual side. The battle will continue until our bodies are changed and we become complete in Christ throughout eternity.

Christ must be the most important person in our lives. He must sit squarely upon the throne of our personal kingdoms. If He is not the most important person in our lives, we will not be effective in bringing our friends, neighbors, and families to personal relationships with him.

Investment of Time

Time is a precious personal commodity! Personal evangelism requires an investment of time. Time must be spent in prayer, preparation and planning to reach people for Christ. This time could be spent doing a variety of other things. Some of these things may be valuable and worthwhile.

To be effective in personal evangelism we must remember at the outset, that it will require our time. We must be willing to commit our time to winning other people to Christ. This means that we willingly limit some of our activities.

Investment of Treasure

Matthew 6:21 reminds us of Jesus' words; *where your treasure is, there is where your heart is also.* Another way to say it; *show me how you spend your money, and I will tell you what truly is important to you*.

If Christ and bringing people to Him through personal evangelism are important to you, then you will be willing to invest your resources in efforts to reach others.

5. Personal Compassion

The Compassion of Christ

Jesus showed tremendous compassion to individuals and multitudes of people.

Matthew 9:36 *But when he saw the multitudes; he was moved with compassion for them, because they were harassed.* (WEB)

Matthew 23:37 *O Jerusalem, Jerusalem, putting to death the prophets, and stoning those who are sent to her! Again and again would I have taken your children to myself as a bird takes her young ones under her wings, and you would not!* (BBE)

John 8:11 *She (woman taken in adultery) said, No man, Lord. And Jesus said unto her, neither do I condemn thee: go, and sin no more.* (KJV)

The Compassion of Paul

Romans 9:3 *For I could wish that myself were accursed from Christ for my brethren, my kinsmen according to the flesh:*(KJV)

We must have the heart of Christ and care deeply for the unsaved world around us. We must see these unsaved people as Christ sees them and care as deeply as Paul cared for them.

We must develop personal compassion, viewing the unsaved world as lost sheep with no sense of direction or shepherd.

6. Personal Prayer

Pray for power from on high.

Acts 1:8 *But ye shall receive power, after that the Holy Ghost is come upon you: and ye shall be witnesses unto me both in Jerusalem, and in all Judaea, and in Samaria, and unto the uttermost part of the earth. (KJV)*

We have *power from on high* available to us. To be effective witnesses we need that power. We should pray and ask the Holy Spirit to overshadow us and help us.

Pray for direction.

Acts 16:9 *And a vision appeared to Paul in the night; There stood a man of Macedonia, and prayed him, saying, come over into Macedonia, and help us.*

(KJV)

Sharing the gospel with others should not be done without a sense of direction. The Holy Spirit, through a vision or dream during the night, gave the apostle Paul direction. God directed Paul to whom the gospel should be shared.

We should pray for God to open doors and guide us to those He would want us to share the gospel. The Holy Spirit will gently help us know when, where, and to whom we should share the gospel. Personal prayer is a pivotal part a personal evangelism

7. Personal Bible Study

God's Word is our chief weapon.

Jeremiah 23:29 *Is not my word like as a fire? Saith the LORD; and like a hammer that breaks the rock in pieces? (KJV)*

God's Word is not optional.

2 Timothy 2:15 Study to show thyself approved unto God, a workman that needeth not to be ashamed, rightly dividing the word of truth. (KJV)

God's Word illuminates His *Good News*.

2 Corinthians *4:6 For God, who commanded the light to shine out of darkness, hath shined in our hearts, to*

give the light of the knowledge of the glory of God in the face of Jesus Christ. (KJV)

8. Personal Dependence

Presence of the Holy Spirit

John 14:16-17 *And I will pray the Father, and he shall give you another Comforter, that he may abide with you forever; Even the Spirit of truth; whom the world cannot receive, because it seeth him not, neither knoweth him: but ye know him; for he dwelleth with you, and shall be in you.* (KJV)

Power of the Holy Spirit

John 15:26 *But when the Comforter is come, whom I will send unto you from the Father, even the Spirit of truth, which proceedeth from the Father, he shall testify of me.* (KJV)

9. Personal Perseverance

Sow the seed.

Ecclesiastes 11:6 *In the morning sow thy seed, and in the evening withhold not thine hand: for thou knowest not whether shall prosper, either this or that, or whether they both shall be alike good. (KJV)*

Remember, our job is not to save anyone. We are *seed sowers*. We are to sow the seeds of the gospel message and trust God to help the seed grow resulting in a great harvest of souls.

Only God knows what kind of soil the seed will fall on. Our job is to plant the seed and leave the rest in the capable hands of the Holy Spirit.

Keep the Faith.

1 Corinthians 15:58 *Therefore, my beloved brethren, be ye stedfast, unmoveable, always abounding in the work of the Lord, forasmuch as ye know that your labor is not in vain in the Lord.* (KJV)

We must remind ourselves that personal evangelism requires three actions:

1. *Planting*
2. *Watering*

3. *Harvesting*.

As personal soul winners we will probably be involved in all three of these.

We are all called to be planters. Sometimes others may do the planting and we are called upon to water the planted seeds. Occasionally we are permitted to be reapers of the harvest. We may be involved in all three at the same time with one or more individuals.

The underlying important thing to remember is that God provides the increase and causes the seeds to develop to maturity and makes them ready for harvesting. We must trust the Lord to handle the harvest and the process leading up to the harvesting.

Our first conference in Eldoret, Kenya in 2012 was held in a tent. I preached and taught for four days on personal evangelism and how to lead others Christ. The week went well and the response was very positive.

My host, Bishop Chris, was very excited about what had taken place. He informed me on Saturday before we returned to America that 43 people had come to a saving knowledge of Christ during the week.

My immediate response was to inquire how that had happened. He told me that 12 people accepted Christ after my Sunday morning message and that many other unsaved people came in off the street and heard the teaching on salvation during the week. The Holy Spirit used the messages to convict their hearts and a total of 43 came to Christ during the week.

I returned to Eldoret the following year for a second conference and we expanded to also include Evangelistic Crusades. We saw another 50 souls come to Christ.

Returning for a third conference in 2014 the tent had been replaced by a nice new church building.

I returned again in 2015 and 2016. The church was experiencing tremendous growth and had expanded to two worship services on Sunday morning.

Bishop Chris expressed his appreciation to me and explained that the key to the growth of the church was personal evangelism and evangelistic crusades.

The key to true growth in our churches is evangelism.

Chapter 6

Sharing The Gospel

Part 1 – Opening the Door

I received word that an accident had occurred a few miles from the church that involved a church member's daughter. I immediately drove to the location and was alarmed to find the car had rolled over and the driver's door was pinned against a light pole.

I knew one of the deputies on

scene and talked with him about what had occurred. He described what had taken place. Shirley had been drinking and lost control of the car causing it to roll over. Her door opened during the rollover.

The car came to rest with Shirley's head pinned between the open door frame and the roof of the car. One more inch and her skull would have been crushed.

I learned that she'd been taken to the emergency room and I drove to the hospital to check on her. I'll tell you what I found and how this sad story unfolds at the end of this chapter.

I believe many people would love to share what Christ has done in their lives with others who desperately need to hear. They are afraid they might embarrass themselves, say something wrong or maybe do damage to the individual or the cause of Christ.

This fear comes from not knowing how to approach people or what to say. I have good news! We can learn how to approach people and what to say.

We can overcome our fears by gaining the knowledge necessary to feel confident that we know what we are doing and how to do it.

Here are Biblical answers to the

two great problems that can keep us from witnessing to others.

<u>Fear</u> – Psalm 34:4; I sought the LORD, and he heard me, and delivered me from all my fears.

<u>Lack of Knowledge</u> – 2 Timothy 2:15 Study to show thyself approved unto God, a workman that needeth not to be ashamed, rightly dividing the word of truth.

How Do I Begin?

1. The Opening Moments

✓ **Greetings** – The conversation should begin with basic greetings. This is a way to open the door and connect to the person to whom you want to share the Gospel.

- ✓ **Give a Compliment**- This will greatly depend on where you are talking with the person or what comes up in the conversation. Notice something that seems to stand out. If you are in their home, notice decorations, furnishings, family pictures, etc. If you are outside their home, notice the lawn, the house, the landscaping, the location, etc. Find something you can compliment and be sincere in your compliment.

- ✓ **Listen Well**- You may learn a great deal about the person and his/her life and circumstances by listening to them. You must discipline yourself and learn to listen rather than just thinking about what you will say next. It is easy to miss something important because you are thinking more about what you will say next rather than listening to what the person is telling you now.

- ✓ **Move to the Center** – Resist the temptation on prolonging an enjoyable conversation at the risk of failing to move on to weightier matters. Remember, this is potentially a matter of life or eternal death for the person you are talking with. Use the conversation as a *springboard* to move to the heart of the reason you are talking with this person.

2. Their Religious Background

Discovering the religious background is important. Many identify themselves with a church, denomination, or a particular faith. Understanding his/her background will help you approach them in a better and more thoughtful way.

You can do this by asking specific questions. The first question that should be asked is; *do you mind if I ask you a question*? This does two things; it alerts them that a question may be coming and it also respects their privacy by asking for permission.

Each question should have purpose and yield information that will help you with your ultimate goal of sharing the gospel of Jesus Christ.

- ✓ **Present Church**- it is important to gain clarity on their present spiritual condition. This begins with a simple question. *Do you have a church you regularly attend*? You may hear responses like; we are members of a certain church, we attend such and such church, and some may be very honest and say we do not attend anywhere right now.

You might use a follow-up question

and ask; *who is the pastor*? You will find out quickly if they are attending church regularly. You should remind yourself whether they attend or do not attend is not the most important issue.

Remember your role. You are an ambassador of Jesus Christ and your purpose is to share your witness for Him. You also represent your church. These are important things to remember.

Do not criticize the person, their church or denomination.

3. Your Church

Only use this section if the person you are talking to has recently visited your church. If the person hasn't visited, then move onto the next section and prepare to ask some piercing questions.

Ask the person how he or she came to visit your church. After learning this, then ask; *what was your impression of our services*? Ask if they noticed anything special or a difference in the service?

Mention the difference is what your folks have experienced through a relationship with Jesus Christ. Explain that Christ gives peace to everyone who seeks Him.

We all are looking for peace. Many people haven't found it though they tried hard and looked at many places.

4. Important Questions

When you reach this point, you are moving into the most serious area of your discussion. You are about to ask some questions that might well impact the individual's eternal destiny.

You should again ask permission to pose certain questions. Begin by asking; *would you mind if I ask you something*? Receiving permission at this point opens the door for weightier questions that will follow.

You are about to move into the spiritual realm, which might determine the eternal destiny of the individual you're talking with. This has been the goal from the very beginning of your conversation.

The next question to ask is; *how is your relationship with the Lord*?

Responses may vary from: I think things are okay, I believe they're pretty good, I'm a good person, etc.

One important thing to remember, your purpose is not to question their relationship the Lord or to affirm it. Your goal is to help them realize their need of the Savior and how they may come to know Him.

A great way to follow up on this question is to say; *let me put it another way, if you were to die right here, right now at this moment, do you know for certain that you would go to be with God in heaven*?

That question is the most important one. It brings into focus the reality of the spiritual condition of the individual you are talking with. You may receive a number of responses such as: I hope so, I would like to think so, I don't know or you may hear a simple no I don't know for sure.

Regardless on the response you receive, this sets the stage for a transition question. You are about to ask permission to share the gospel. The next question opens the door for you to share

Jesus Christ who is the way, the truth and the life.

You are about to move into the Scriptures because it is *the truth that sets men and women free*. The word of God brings saving faith. *Faith comes by hearing, and hearing by the word of God.*

The piercing question that should then be asked is; *may I share with you how I came to know for sure and how you can also*?

I've asked this question to many people and I have never had anyone tell me that they did not want me to share this with them. The key is to make sure the timing is right to ask this question.

Once you've asked this question and received an answer, you're ready to move forward with sharing Scriptures from the book of Romans. You are about to help the individual understand how he or she can know for certain if they died before they leave you that day, they will go to be with the Lord in heaven.

Now back to Shirley. She was in her late twenties and her life was mess. Shirley was on her second marriage and she was with another man when the accident occurred.

Her husband was a good man and was hard at work at his mechanic's job while his wife was being unfaithful to him resulting in crashing the car he'd bought for her.

Shirley's father met me at the door of the emergency room with tears streaming down his face. I could hear cursing and yelling coming from the treatment rooms nearby.

Preacher Harris, Shirley is drunk but they tell me she only has minor injuries. They will keep her overnight and she should be released in a day or so. I'm afraid this will not be a good time for you to try to talk with her. I'm embarrassed because of the way she is acting. Maybe you could come back in the morning?

I shook his hand and placed my other hand on his shoulder and assured him that I loved and cared about him, Shirley and his entire family and I would be glad to return the next morning.

I did return and will never forget our conversation. Her husband was at her bedside sticking by his wife even though he knew she'd been unfaithful to him. I recalled the accident and the fact that God had spared her life the day before. I asked her the all-important question; *If you'd died in that accident, do you know for certain that you would have gone to meet the Lord in heaven?*

She quickly changed the subject

saying *the people over there at your church are all hypocrites. I'm young and I have some things I want to do before I get saved*. I reminded her that God had given her a second chance and she should take advantage of it. She was more concerned about the small area of hair that had been shaved from her head than with her spiritual condition.

Her father passed away some months later and I preached his funeral. Shirley attended our church occasionally after that and I remember the last service she attended. I preached a strong but compassionate salvation message and God impressed me to make a statement during the invitation.

I said *this might be your last opportunity to accept Christ as your Savior.* I didn't know how prophetic this would be for Shirley.

I glanced at the clock when the phone rang waking me at 2:00 a.m. Phone calls at that time of the morning are never good, especially for a pastor. The voice on the other end of the line was Shirley's husband.

His voice was trembling and he was crying. *Preacher Harris, Shirley just shot herself and she's dead. I don't know what to do.* He went on to explain that Shirley had been out drinking that night and they'd gotten into an argument when she came home. *She took my 12 gage shot gun, put the barrel under her chin and pulled the trigger. I heard the shot in the front yard. When I ran out of the house I couldn't even recognize her.*

I told him he needed to call the police immediately. He then asked me to please go and tell Shirley's mom. I called a neighbor family who were church members and they graciously agreed to come and stay with our two children while my wife and I made the short drive to Hazel's home.

I knocked and eventually she opened the door. I asked Hazel to sit down in a chair and I knelt in front of her and took both her hands. *I have some bad news.* She began to cry and said *Oh no, it's Jo Ann.* Jo Ann was her other daughter. *I'm sorry Hazel, it's Shirley* I said.

I can still hear what Hazel said as she yelled, *I can hear her (Shirley) screaming in hell!*

Not everyone will respond to the gospel. Our job is not to save people but to offer them the free gift of salvation. They must make the choice. Just a reminder of how serious that matter of eternity is and we must do all we can to share the gospel with others.

Chapter 7

Sharing the Gospel

Part 2 - The Biblical Plan For Salvation

After prayer, we were on our way to talk with a man who had visited our church the previous Sunday. He raised his hand indicating he did not know Christ and that he'd like for me to pray for him.

Randy had accompanied me on a number of visits in the past and had first hand experience of watching me lead others to Christ. We made our way down the highway on our way to our soul-winning destination.

This visit would be quite different from the others that Randy and I had made. Our conversation shifted from our normal chitchat to something more serious. I paused for a moment and then I said to Randy...... I'll tell you at the end of this chapter what I said and what happened during our visit.

We must remember that we cannot save anyone. The gospel is the power of God that brings salvation. Our job is to communicate the gospel message clearly and effectively, offering a choice to those who hear it.

All Are Sinners

Before one can be found, one must first become lost. It is imperative that we help individuals understand that all of us sin and fall short of God's standard and what he requires. The best verse that I have found to illustrate that point is Romans 3:23. The King James Version says:

> Romans 3:23 - *For all have sinned and come short of the glory of God.*

When we share the gospel we begin by quoting or reading this verse to the person.

Remember we have just asked the individual if we might share with him how we came to know for sure that if we died right now we could go to be with the Lord in heaven and how he can know also. We are beginning the process.

So begin by saying: The Bible tells us in Romans 3:23 *that all have sinned and fall short of the glory of God*. What that verse means is that all of us are sinners. That means I sinned, you sinned, and every person who has ever lived has sinned. No matter how good a person may be, it is impossible to be perfect and to be good enough to go to heaven.

I like to use the illustration of sawing a board. If the board is intended to be used for a specific purpose and must be an exact length and I cut the board too short, then no matter how hard I try I will not be able to make the board fit its intended use.

We are like that board. We have an intended use and purpose for which God created each of us. On our own, we will never be able fulfill the purpose God intended for us because we do not have the ability within ourselves.

So all of us fall short of God's standard of perfection because we have sinned. *All have sinned and fall short of the glory God demands*.

God Loves Us

The next step down the Romans Road of the gospel of Jesus Christ is to help individuals understand that even while we are sinners, God loves us. He loves us just as we are and wants to help us with what we can become.

The next verse I would suggest using is Romans 5:8 *But God commendeth His love toward us, in that, while we were yet sinners, Christ died for us*.

Tell them God loves everyone. That He loves us even while we are sinners. He demonstrated that love by the death of His son Jesus Christ on the cross to pay the debt for our sins. He loved us so much that Jesus died in our place.

Tell the individual; *this means that God loves you and that Jesus died for you*.

The Penalty for Sin

Why did Jesus die on the cross for us?

Next, you should use Romans 6:23. Say to the person; *the Bible says in Romans 6:23 that the wages of sin is death*.

Explain that our sins accumulate over a period of time, much like when we receive a paycheck at the end of the week or the month. We receive our wages based on the work we have done.

The same is true with our sins. Because of our sins, we deserve payment for our wrongdoing in violating God's laws. The Bible tells us in this verse that *the wages we have earned is death*. We deserve and have earned death because of our sins.

Jesus died on the cross freely receiving the wages and punishment that you and I deserved.

The Gift of Eternal Life

Move quickly to the second part of Romans 6:23. Tell him; *we understand that we deserve spiritual death, but the good news is that Christ died in our place and offers us the gift of eternal life*.

The Bible says in the last part of verse 23, *but the gift of God is eternal life through Jesus Christ our Lord*. We do not deserve it but God freely offers this gift of eternal life to us.

A good way to illustrate this is to compare it to a Christmas gift. Tell him; *when my family takes the time, effort, and expense to purchase a gift for me*. *They place the gift in front of me on Christmas morning. This is a gift that has been offered to me.*

Jesus Christ offers the gift of eternal life to us. It costs us nothing yet cost him everything. Even though the gift has been offered I must choose to receive it for it to truly be mine.

How can we receive this gift?

Receive the Gift of Eternal Life

The verses I use at this point are Romans 10:8–10. The Bible tells us that: *if we believe that Jesus Christ died and rose from the dead for our sins and we confess our sins and ask him to forgive us then we will be saved*.

Explain that all he has to do is believe that Jesus Christ can save him and ask Christ to come into his heart and a change his life. Explain that we believe in our hearts and talk to God with our mouths.

That's all there is to it. That's all he has to do!

God's Promise

Romans 10:13 carries a tremendous promise for every person. It says that; *anyone who calls upon the name of the Lord shall be saved*. This promise should be conveyed to the individual.

I usually state something like this; *this verse doesn't say you might be saved or you could be saved, it says you WILL BE SAVED*!

The Important Decision

This is an important moment! You've shared the good news of Jesus Christ. You've shown the individual how he can receive this wonderful free gift of salvation.

You are ready to press for a decision. Say to the individual, *this means if you will call out to the Lord, He will hear you and He will save you. You can do this right now, right here*.

Wouldn't you like to ask Christ to come into your heart right now?

If the person says yes, then move to the next step, which is prayer.

The Prayer For Salvation

The thought of praying may be scary and a bit intimidating for individuals who are not used to praying. So a gentle hand will be helpful in walking the individual through the sinner's prayer.

Tell the individual that all he has to do is tell the Lord:

- *I am sorry for my sins.*
- *I believe You can save me.*
- *Please come into my heart and change my life.*

Tell him that's all he has to do.

- *Ask if he would like to pray out loud or silently*. (Most will want to pray silently.)

- Then say something like; *you pray and then I'll pray*.
- *Please say Amen out loud so I'll know when you've finished then I'll pray*.
- When he finishes praying and says Amen, respond by saying: *Now I'll pray.*

The Prayer for Assurance

Your goal at this moment is to help the individual gain assurance that he has done what the Bible said he needed to do. Now he can know for sure that he is saved and on his way to heaven.

How can you do this?

- You should pray an abbreviated prayer out loud, restating the plan of salvation reaffirming what he (call his name in the prayer) has just done, concluding with your own Amen when you are finished.
- Look at him and ask; *how are you feeling*?
- Then remind him that he has done what the Scriptures said he needed to do in order to be saved.
- Ask him again; *do you know for certain now that you*

could go to be with the Lord in heaven if you died right here and right now?

- Then say; *always remember this day when you and I prayed together and you asked Christ to come into your heart.*
- Then ask him to write down in his Bible today's date with a note saying *this was the day that Jesus Christ came into my heart and saved me.*
- Encourage the person to be in church on Sunday morning at a certain time. *Reassure*

him that you will be waiting for him at the door and you will sit with him during the service. (Have someone else prepared to sit with him if you will be preaching, or have other responsibilities that will prevent you.)

- Next, *encourage him to be prepared to come forward* during the invitation time in church on Sunday so you can pray with him.
    - Explain exactly how it will unfold so you can remove the fear of the

unknown.

- Explain the importance of making the decision public.
- Describe how Jesus always called those who would follow him publicly.
- Explain how this will help him and how he will benefit from this step.
    - For *his benefit* – it seals the decision in his mind.

- For the *church's benefit* – so they will know to pray for him.

A Bible

Ask the individual if he has a Bible. If he has a Bible, encourage him to begin immediately reading the Gospel of John. If he doesn't have one, then find a way to get one into his hands as soon as possible.

Follow Up

There are many good discipleship follow up programs and a variety of follow up materials. Since this book's main focus is personal evangelism and how to lead others to Jesus Christ, time and space will not permit an in-depth discussion of discipleship and follow-up materials.

Now back to our story...

Our conversation moved into more serious territory. I paused for a moment then said to Randy; *I want you to take the lead during our visit tonight.* There was another pause in our conversation and Randy replied; *I'm not sure I'm ready to do this.* I reassured him that he was ready and the Holy Spirit would help him.

The gentleman was expecting us and knew why we came to see him.

Randy was a little nervous as we began the conversation. He asked the man; *Steve, are you saved?*

Randy looked over at me as soon as the words left his lips. He remembered that you never ask if someone is saved. Many people have a false understanding of what *being saved* means. They may have their own standard by which they measure what being right with God means to them.

Randy quickly pivoted to the piercing questions that opened the door to confront Steve with his lost condition. Steve didn't accept Christ that night, but he understood where he was spiritually, what he needed, and how he could receive the free gift of salvation.

Randy did a great job that night and there are lessons we can learn from his experience. You must be willing to take the first step and talk with one person about Christ.

Personal evangelism is a learning experience. The more you practice it, the better you become at it. You will make miscues and you learn from each one. The Holy Spirit will guide you and help you.

Randy went on to become a prolific soul winner, deacon and leader in the church.

Chapter 8

Using Common Sense in Personal Evangelism

There's an old expression *practice makes perfect*. Souls are too important for us not to be prepared when we talk with individuals about their spiritual condition.

I began a practice in my first church in Ahoskie, NC that I've repeated in each of the four churches I've pastored. It's been so effective that I thought I'd share it here.

I'll describe the practice at the end of this chapter.

Now that we've gained an understanding of how to lead others to a saving knowledge of Jesus Christ, there are some practical common sense principles we should remember.

Below you will find 10 principles to remember as you reach out to share the gospel with others.

1. We must *be good listeners*.

We must believe that listening is important. We should understand the difference between hearing words and listening.

- Hearing is receiving stimuli over auditory paths.

- Listening involves not only hearing, but also interpretation, evaluation, and responding to what is said.

- We must listen closely to what individuals tell us when we are attempting to lead them to Christ. We can pick up on small things that will aid us in our conversation and also might be a key to winning them to Christ.

2. We must *sidestep diversions and avoid arguments*.

You may be asked questions about

specific things, if they are right or wrong. You may be asked other questions that could divert your discussion away from the goal of leading individuals to Christ.

When you are asked these kinds of questions, the best response that I have found is to simply say; *that's a good question, we'll get back to that later, but in the meantime* – then return to the place in the conversation where you were before the question was asked.

Do not allow yourself to be pulled off track and away from the important matter at hand. That matter is the eternal destiny of the individual you are talking with.

Do not allow yourself to be drawn into an argument. Listen for something you can agree on. Let the Holy Spirit win the person and stay away from arguments.

3. We must *avoid judgmental attitudes*.

- Do not register shock by a person's lifestyle. You must love sinners and remind yourself that God loves them where they are in their lives. It's God's job to take them to where they need to be.
- Do not rebuke the person but try and help him find the new lifestyle that

only Christ can give.

4. <u>Observe Common Courtesies</u>.

- Pronounce the person's name correctly.
- Ask permission for personal questions.
- Respect a person's space.
- Be conscious of children. Talk to them and also complement them to their parents.
- Be considerate of the person's previous plans.
- Do not talk or stay too long.
- Do not talk when someone else is talking.

- Check your shoes and make sure the bottoms are clean before entering the home.
- Be cautious about interrupting a special TV program.

5. Avoid *manipulating the person*.

Make sure the person really knows what he is doing and give him the opportunity to say no if he is not ready to accept Christ at that moment.

6. *Use the Bible wisely*.

- Use a small New Testament.

Carrying a big Bible when trying to

witness to someone may turn him off.

- Purchase a few New Testaments and keep them on hand to give away.

7. *DO NOT criticize others*.

Never criticize another person, church, pastor or denomination. Enough said!

8. *NEVER embarrass the person*.

Think before you speak. Put yourself in the other person's place and think about how you might receive what you are about to say. Never do anything or say anything that might embarrass the person.

9. ***Leave a good impression*.**

- Especially if the person does not accept Christ.
- We want the opportunity to talk with him again.
- We do not want to close the door on someone else that might be able to win him to Christ later.

10. ***Good grooming is important*.**

- Shower
- Brush teeth
- Comb hair
- Carry breath mints

I'd just completed several weeks of teaching my approach to winning people one-on-one to Jesus Christ. I decided that it might be good to give an example of the approach to my people. We set up a living room scene on a Wednesday night in the auditorium.

Our school principal, Kyle, served as the man I would visit and share Christ with. I knocked on the door and he invited me in. We had discussed in detail our goal for what we hoped to accomplish.

We made our interaction as real as possible. I went through the approach step by step sharing how this man could know that things were right between him and the Lord and that if he died where he was sitting, he could know for certain that he could go to be with the Lord in heaven.

Our people were able to see the plan in action and understand how it might work for them. I arranged for Kyle to ask questions that others sometimes ask in an effort to throw me off message and I showed how to respond and stay on message.

Using this role-playing approach proved to be a great help to others. I repeated this a number of times with different churches I pastored and also in personal evangelism conferences I've conducted.

It works well in large and small group settings.

www.ingramcontent.com/pod-product-compliance
Lightning Source LLC
Chambersburg PA
CBHW071539040426
42452CB00008B/1064

9780997281644